NUMBERS EXPLAINED

NUMBERS EXPLAINED

Understanding the Book and Its Message for Today

Samuel Whitaker

Part of the Bible for Modern Life Series

Ascent Press

Published by
Ascent Press

ISBN: 978-1-972885-05-5
Printed in the United States of America

First Edition 2026

For those seeking clarity in the ancient words of Scripture.

CONTENTS

Introduction   1

Chapter 1 — The Human Question   5

Chapter 2 — Orientation   13

Chapter 3 — The World Behind the Book   23

Chapter 4 — The Story or Flow   33

Chapter 5 — Key Themes   43

Chapter 6 — Where People Get It Wrong   53

Chapter 7 — What It Means for Modern Life   63

Chapter 8 — Modern Reflection   73

Chapter 9 — Reflection Questions   83

Chapter 10 — Five Lessons   93

Closing Reflection   107

Disclaimer

This book provides an interpretive overview of the biblical text using historical scholarship and modern analysis tools. It is intended to help readers understand the themes, context, and message of the biblical narrative and is not intended to replace personal study of Scripture

Introduction

Why Numbers Still Matters

Numbers is the book of the wilderness — not the wilderness as romantic metaphor for spiritual searching, but the wilderness as consequence. Israel had been liberated from Egypt, ratified the covenant at Sinai, received the law through Moses, and constructed the tabernacle according to divine specification. They had everything they needed to enter the land they had been promised. And then, standing at its border, they refused to go in.

The result was forty years of wandering. An entire generation died in the desert — not because the wilderness was inescapable but because the people could not bring themselves to trust the God who had already demonstrated, repeatedly and dramatically, that he was capable of doing what he had promised. Numbers is the honest record of that failure: the complaints, the rebellions, the longing for Egypt, the mutinies against Moses, the moments when the community came within a breath of dissolving entirely. It is not a comfortable book. It was not designed to be.

The English title comes from the two census counts that frame the book — one taken at Sinai before the journey resumes, one taken on the plains of Moab a generation later as a new community prepares to enter what the first refused. But the Hebrew title is more accurate: Bemidbar, meaning in the wilderness. That is where the book lives — in the long middle between the promise and its fulfillment, in the space where faith is tested not by the dramatic crises of exodus and conquest but by the grinding daily question of whether the God who brought you this far can be trusted to bring you the rest of the way.

What makes the wilderness of Numbers so theologically significant is precisely that it was unnecessary. The distance from Sinai to the land of Canaan was not forty years by any geographic reckoning. The journey that Numbers describes could have been completed in weeks. The forty years were not the natural duration of the trip. They were the consequence of the community's decision at Kadesh Barnea — the refusal to trust the God who had organized, equipped, and led them to the threshold of everything he had promised. The wilderness is not the setting of the story. It is the punishment for the story's central failure, and the book's insistence on inhabiting that punishment honestly, across all thirty-six chapters, is what gives it its distinctive theological weight.

Numbers addresses the most honest dimension of spiritual life: not the mountaintop moments but the years between them. It is the book for those who know what God has done and still struggle to trust what he will do — who have witnessed faithfulness in the past and find it insufficient anchor for the fears of the present. Every generation of the covenant community has lived in some version of the wilderness that Numbers describes, and every generation has needed the book's unflinching account of what unbelief costs and what persistent divine faithfulness looks like in the face of it.

The chapters that follow explore the historical world of Numbers, the structure of its argument, the major themes that run through its wilderness narrative, the ways it has been misread, and the specific ways it continues to address communities navigating their own long middles. The goal throughout is not to make Numbers easier to receive but to make it possible to receive it honestly — as the demanding, realistic, ultimately hopeful account of a God who does not abandon the people who fail him, and of a people who discovered, at great cost, that the wilderness was never the destination.

Numbers also speaks with unusual directness to communities that are navigating institutional complexity — the specific challenge of maintaining a coherent identity and a coherent mission across the kind of structural complexity that a large community in motion inevitably produces. The census lists and administrative regulations that modern readers tend to skip are the evidence of a community that took its organizational life seriously as a dimension of its covenant faithfulness. The arrangement of the camp, the assignment of tribal responsibilities, the careful specification of who carries what and who marches where — all of this is the organizational infrastructure of a community that understood its movement through the wilderness as a mission rather than a migration. The attention Numbers pays to this infrastructure is not a distraction from its theological concerns. It is the expression of them: the conviction that the God who called this community to its destination is a God who is interested in the specific, practical, organizational dimensions of how the community moves toward it.

Chapter 1

The Human Question

*"The LORD said to Moses in the wilderness of Sinai... Take a
census of the whole Israelite community."*
--- Numbers 1:1-2 (NIV)

The Experience of the Long Middle

Every serious human life eventually discovers the territory that
Numbers describes: the long middle between a genuine promise
and its fulfillment, the stretch of time between when you were told
what would be and when it finally arrives — and the question that
the length of that stretch generates about whether the promise
was real, whether you heard it correctly, or whether something
you have done has disqualified you from receiving it. The
Israelites in the wilderness did not doubt that God existed. They
had seen the plagues. They had walked through the sea on dry
ground. They had heard the voice at Sinai and eaten the manna
that appeared each morning on the ground. The question was not
whether God was real. It was whether the God who was real was
going to do what he had said — whether the land that had been
promised was actually going to be given, whether the journey that
kept extending was ever going to end.

This is a more specific and more searching form of the
question of faith than the question of God's existence, and it is the
question that Numbers is organized around. The existence
question can be settled by evidence. The long-middle question
cannot. It is settled only by the willingness to keep moving in the
direction of the promise when the evidence of immediate

experience suggests that the promise is not coming — when the wilderness goes on longer than expected, when the manna that was miraculous in the first weeks has become tedious in the fortieth year, when the community around you is losing its will to believe and the loss is contagious. The Israelites failed this question, and the failure cost them everything. Numbers is the record of the failure and the ongoing divine faithfulness that the failure did not terminate. Both are essential to what the book has to say.

The long middle is not a unique feature of the biblical wilderness account. It is the normal condition of every serious vocational, relational, and spiritual commitment that any honest human life involves. The researcher who spends a decade on a question that does not yield its answer on the expected timeline. The couple who entered marriage with genuine promises and discovered that the life they promised each other requires more years of difficult work before it becomes what they intended it to be. The community of faith that received a genuine vision of what it could become and has been navigating the distance between that vision and present reality for longer than anyone expected. Numbers is the biblical book that most directly addresses this condition because it is the book that most completely inhabits it — not as a brief episode to be overcome but as the primary territory of the covenant community's life across forty years of documented experience.

The Exhaustion of Sustained Faith

The second human question that Numbers presses is the one about the cost of sustained faith over time — the specific exhaustion that comes not from a single dramatic crisis but from the accumulation of ordinary days in which the promise seems no closer than it did the day before. This is a different kind of challenge than the challenge of the crisis. Crises concentrate attention and generate urgency. They produce the clarity of extreme circumstances in which the choice between trust and despair is obvious and the stakes are impossible to miss. The wilderness does neither. It produces a slow grinding of hope against the indifference of ordinary days, and the grinding is more dangerous than the crisis because it operates below the threshold of drama and is therefore harder to recognize as the threat it is.

The Israelites in Numbers do not primarily lose their faith in a single dramatic moment of apostasy, though there are such moments. They lose it gradually, complaint by complaint, through the cumulative weight of a journey that keeps going longer than they expected and a God whose provision, though real, has become so familiar as to seem insufficient. The manna is still arriving every morning. The pillar of cloud and fire is still moving ahead of them. But what was miraculous has become routine, and what is routine is no longer enough to sustain the belief that the promise will ultimately be kept. This is the exhaustion of sustained faith that Numbers diagnoses: not the dramatic failure of courage at a single moment but the slow erosion of trust across the long middle, complaint by complaint, until the accumulated weight of ordinary days has produced a community that can no longer believe its way forward.

The modern reader who has navigated their own version of the long middle — the sustained illness that does not resolve, the marriage that requires years of hard work before it becomes what it was promised to be, the vocation that demands decades of faithfulness before it produces the fruit it was supposed to produce — will recognize the territory Numbers describes with an accuracy that more dramatic biblical narratives do not quite capture. Numbers is the book for the ordinary wilderness, and its diagnosis of what that wilderness does to faith is more useful to most readers than any number of accounts of dramatic crisis and deliverance.

There is a specific spiritual danger in the exhaustion of sustained faith that Numbers documents but rarely names explicitly, and that deserves naming here: the danger of gratitude fatigue. The manna was genuinely miraculous. The community ate it every morning for forty years, and at some point the miracle became the expectation, and the expectation became the resentment when the provision did not exceed the expected minimum. This is not ingratitude in the simple sense. It is the specific exhaustion that extended dependence produces in human beings who were designed for arrival, not for indefinite transit. Numbers does not condemn this exhaustion. It records it honestly and shows what happens when the exhaustion is allowed to interpret the provision as inadequate rather than as the sustaining faithfulness of a God who is keeping the community alive until the destination is reached.

The Question of Communal Faith and Contagion

Numbers also presses a third human question that individual accounts of faith and doubt rarely address with equal directness: the question of what happens when the community around you is losing its faith and the loss is contagious. The Israelites in the wilderness did not doubt in isolation. They doubted together — in the camps, around the fires, in the conversations that spread from tent to tent until what had begun as one family's complaint had become the whole community's crisis. The spies who returned from Canaan with a discouraging report did not simply express their own fear. They created it in those who heard them, and the fear they created was more powerful than the confidence that Caleb and Joshua tried to counter it with. The ten outvoted the two, and the community's collective failure of faith became the sentence that forty years of wilderness would fulfill.

This is the human question of communal faith: what do you do when the people around you cannot believe, and when their inability is actively working against your own capacity to trust? It is a question that every member of every community of faith navigates in some form — in the congregation where the predominant mood is cynicism rather than expectation, in the family where the habit of complaint has become so entrenched that hope sounds naive, in the organization where the accumulated failures of the past have produced a collective inability to believe in the possibility of anything different. Numbers addresses this question not by minimizing its difficulty but by naming its consequences with unusual honesty.

At the same time, Numbers does not allow communal failure to be the final word. Caleb and Joshua believed when the rest of the community could not, and their belief was remembered and rewarded across forty years of wilderness that they did not deserve to be in. The community's failure did not extinguish the possibility of individual faithfulness within it, and the individual faithfulness of those who believed against the communal grain was preserved and honored by the God who had been doubted. Numbers holds both realities simultaneously: the real consequences of communal failure and the real possibility of faithfulness within a failing community.

The Longing to Go Back

Perhaps the most honest human question that Numbers presses is the one that the Israelites voice most consistently and most embarrassingly throughout their wilderness years: the longing to return to Egypt. Not the real Egypt — the Egypt of slavery and oppression and the systematic destruction of their children. The remembered Egypt of leeks and onions and fish and cucumbers, the Egypt that the wilderness has transformed in memory into a place of adequate provision compared to the arid uncertainty of the desert road. When the manna has grown tedious and the water is scarce and the promised land is still somewhere over the horizon, the human capacity for nostalgic revision of even the most painful past is fully on display in Numbers. We remember Egypt, the people say. We had fish there. We had vegetables. Here there is nothing — nothing except this manna.

The longing to go back is one of the most persistent features of human psychology in every era, and Numbers addresses it with unusual directness by showing it in its most extreme and most self-defeating form. The Israelites are not longing for a better version of where they are. They are longing for the slavery from which they were liberated, and they are doing so because the freedom they were given requires more of them — more trust, more patience, more sustained movement in the direction of a promise they cannot yet see fulfilled — than the slavery did. Slavery at least provided the illusion of certainty. Freedom in the wilderness provides provision without security, direction without arrival, and the ongoing requirement to trust a God whose promises keep proving more demanding than expected.

The modern equivalent of this longing is not usually the desire to return to literal slavery. It is the desire to return to the familiar dysfunction that at least had the virtue of being known — the bad relationship that was at least predictable, the unfulfilling job that at least provided certainty, the limited life that at least did not require the risk of trusting something larger than oneself. Numbers names this longing for what it is — not an innocent desire for comfort but a failure of the faith that genuine freedom requires — and it presses the question that the longing generates: what would it mean to stop looking back and trust the God who is ahead?

The Shape of What Follows

These dimensions — the experience of the long middle between promise and fulfillment, the exhaustion of sustained faith across ordinary days, the challenge of communal doubt and its contagion, and the persistent longing to return to what was known rather than trust what has been promised — are not separate topics that Numbers handles in separate sections. They are angles on the single central question that the book asks from its first census to its final plains-of-Moab encampment: what does it mean to be the people of God in the wilderness, and what is required to keep moving in the direction of a promise that has not yet been fully received?

The chapters that follow examine the historical world that produced Numbers, the literary structure that organizes its wilderness narrative, the major themes that run through its accounts of complaint and rebellion and divine response, the ways it has been misread across centuries of reception, and the specific ways it continues to address communities navigating their own long middles. The goal throughout is not to make the wilderness experience of Numbers more comfortable than it was but to make it possible to receive it more honestly — as the book of a God who remained faithful to a people who largely did not, and who kept the promise alive across forty years of the community's most sustained and most consequential failure to believe it.

Chapter 2

Orientation

"The LORD spoke to Moses in the tent of meeting in the
wilderness of Sinai."
--- Numbers 1:1

A Book for a People in Motion

Numbers was written for a community that was moving — or
supposed to be. The entire book is set in transit: the Israelites
have left Sinai and are making their way, however fitfully and
however faithfully, toward the land that has been promised to
them since the days of Abraham. Unlike Leviticus, which is almost
entirely stationary — a community encamped at the foot of a
mountain receiving instruction for a way of life not yet being lived
— Numbers is a travel narrative organized around the movement
of a people from one place to another and the repeated failures
that extend what should have been a short journey into a forty-
year ordeal. The community for whom Numbers was preserved
and transmitted was a community that needed to understand its
own history of failure honestly and to receive, through that honest
engagement, both the warning of what unbelief costs and the
sustaining assurance that the God who called the community to
the journey did not abandon it when the journey went wrong.

That community was also, in every subsequent generation, a
community that recognized its own experience in the wilderness
narrative. The rabbis who transmitted the Torah understood
Numbers as the most searching mirror available for the covenant
community's self-examination — the book that asked, in narrative

form, the question that every generation of the community had to answer for itself: will you trust the God who has brought you this far, or will you repeat the failure of those who could not? The question has not lost its urgency across the millennia that separate the original wilderness community from the communities that read Numbers today.

The book's setting in motion also means that its legislation has a different character from the legislation of Leviticus. Where Leviticus legislates for a settled community organized around a permanent sanctuary, Numbers legislates for a community on the road — addressing the specific legal questions that arise when the normal structures of settled life are unavailable, when property disputes, inheritance questions, and leadership challenges must be resolved in the field rather than in established courts, and when the relationship between the community and its God must be maintained through the portable sanctuary that travels with it rather than through the fixed institutions of a settled religious life. The legislation of Numbers is situational in a way that Leviticus's legislation is not, and understanding this situational character is essential for reading its legal sections with the attention they deserve.

Authorship and the Mosaic Tradition

Like the rest of the Torah, Numbers does not identify its author by name within the text. It presents itself as the record of events and divine speech mediated through Moses — the LORD spoke to Moses is the formula that introduces most of its major legislative and narrative sections, and Moses is the central human figure throughout. The traditional attribution of Numbers, along with the rest of the Torah, to Mosaic authorship has been the dominant view in Jewish and Christian history and remains the position of many communities of faith today.

Modern scholarship has approached the question of authorship differently, identifying within Numbers the traces of multiple source traditions — the priestly material associated with the sanctuary and the Aaronic priesthood, the older narrative material whose style and concerns differ from the priestly passages, and a series of ancient poems and oracles embedded in the text whose origins appear to predate the surrounding narrative. The Balaam oracles of chapters twenty-two through twenty-four, for instance, are widely regarded as among the oldest poetry in the Hebrew Bible. The Song of the Well in chapter twenty-one, the Book of the Wars of the LORD referenced in the same chapter, and the various battle poetry embedded in the narrative all suggest that Numbers incorporates material from multiple periods and traditions.

As with the other books of the Torah, the question of compositional history, while genuinely interesting, does not determine the theological significance of the content. Whatever the process by which Numbers reached its final form, the book as it stands is a coherent theological argument about the wilderness period — about what happened between Sinai and the plains of Moab, why it happened, and what it means for the community that inherits the account. The theological argument is what every reader must engage, and it does not depend on settling the historical questions that scholars continue to debate.

The Structure of the Book

Numbers divides naturally into four recognizable sections organized around geography and generation. The first section, covering chapters one through ten, is set at Sinai and consists of the preparations for departure: the census of the fighting men, the arrangement of the camp around the tabernacle, the consecration of the Levites, the observance of the second Passover, and the final divine instructions before the journey resumes. The community is organized, equipped, and ready to move. The narrative is orderly, the tone is expectant, and the reader who has come through Exodus and Leviticus has every reason to expect that what follows will be the triumphant entry into the promised land.

The second section, covering chapters eleven through twenty-five, is the longest and the most theologically dense. It is the account of the wilderness wandering proper — the complaints about food and water, the rebellion of Miriam and Aaron against Moses, the catastrophic failure of nerve at Kadesh Barnea when the spies return from Canaan, the forty-year sentence that failure produces, the challenges to Moses's leadership from Korah and his allies, the deaths of Miriam and Aaron, Moses's own disqualifying act at Meribah, the bronze serpent, and the Balaam narrative. This section is the heart of the book — the extended, honest, painful account of what a community looks like when it consistently fails to trust the God who has called it forward.

The third section, covering chapters twenty-six through thirty-six, marks the transition to a new generation. A second census is taken — this one of a community that has replaced the generation that died in the wilderness, a community that has not experienced the exodus firsthand but that has inherited both the promise and the responsibility to receive it. The preparations for entering the land begin in earnest: the distribution of the land is planned, the daughters of Zelophehad establish the principle of female inheritance, Joshua is commissioned as Moses's successor, and a series of laws and instructions is given to prepare the new generation for settled life in the land their parents refused to enter.

The transition between the second and third sections is worth pausing over, because it is not marked with dramatic ceremony or theological fanfare. The generation simply dies, one by one, across the chapters, and a new generation appears in its place. Numbers records this transition with the same matter-of-fact honesty it brings to everything else: the sentence was pronounced, the sentence was served, the community continues. The lack of drama in the transition is itself theologically significant. The mission does not depend on the generation that failed. It continues through and beyond them, carried by the God who made the promise and who is entirely capable of finding another generation willing to receive what the first refused.

The Portrait of Moses in Numbers

Numbers contains the most fully developed and most humanly complex portrait of Moses in the entire Torah. The Moses of Numbers is not the heroic liberator of Exodus or the authoritative lawgiver of Leviticus and Deuteronomy. He is a leader navigating an impossible situation — a man called to bring a community to a destination that the community consistently refuses to move toward, whose own leadership is repeatedly challenged by the people he is trying to lead, and who ultimately fails in a moment of uncharacteristic anger that costs him the one thing he most wanted: to enter the land himself.

The portrait is remarkable for its unflinching honesty about its subject's limitations. Moses in Numbers is exhausted. At the moment of the people's loudest complaint about food, he tells God that he cannot carry this community alone — that the burden is too heavy, that he would rather die than continue under its weight. He is challenged by his own sister and brother. He is challenged by Korah and two hundred and fifty community leaders who question whether his authority is genuinely divine rather than self-appointed. He strikes the rock at Meribah in a moment of frustrated anger rather than speaking to it as God commanded, and the consequence is final: he will see the promised land from a distance but will not enter it.

This portrait is not a failure of heroic narrative. It is the specific and irreplaceable contribution that Numbers makes to the Torah's account of human leadership under divine calling. The greatest leader Israel ever had was brought to exhaustion, challenged, and ultimately disqualified by a single moment of failure — and yet the mission continued, the promise was kept, and the land was entered by those who came after. Numbers insists that the mission is not the leader's property. It belongs to the God who called it, and its completion does not depend on the leader's unbroken faithfulness.

The Role of the Wilderness in the Torah's Argument

The wilderness in Numbers is not simply the geographical setting for the events the book describes. It is a theological category — the space between the promise and its fulfillment, the period of testing and formation that stands between liberation and arrival, the place where the character of the covenant community is revealed under conditions that cannot be managed or controlled. In the wilderness there is no Egypt to rely on and no settled land to enjoy. There is only the daily provision of the God who has promised to bring his people through, and the daily choice of whether to receive that provision with trust or to meet it with complaint.

The Torah as a whole is organized around the tension between promise and fulfillment, and Numbers is the book that occupies the most uncomfortable position in that tension. Genesis establishes the promise. Exodus enacts the liberation that begins the journey toward its fulfillment. Leviticus provides the instruction for the holy life the fulfilled promise requires. Deuteronomy revisits the law and the covenant on the eve of entry. Numbers is the book that sits in the middle of all of this — the honest account of what happens in the space between the beginning of the journey and its completion, when the community discovers that trusting the promise is harder than celebrating it.

18

The Literary Character of Numbers

Numbers is the most formally diverse book in the Torah. It contains census lists and travel itineraries, priestly legislation and narrative complaint, divine speeches and ancient poetry, legal precedents established by specific cases and oracles delivered by a foreign prophet. This diversity reflects the range of the wilderness experience it is recording — the administrative requirements of a community on the move, the theological crises that the movement generates, the legal questions that arise in the absence of settled institutions, and the ancient poetry that the community carried with it as the cultural memory of what God had done.

The Balaam narrative of chapters twenty-two through twenty-four is the most literarily distinctive section of the book and one of the most unusual passages in the entire Hebrew Bible. A Gentile prophet hired to curse Israel ends up blessing it four times despite the best efforts of the Moabite king who hired him, in a narrative that combines comedy, pathos, a talking donkey, and some of the most theologically significant poetry in the Torah. The oracles Balaam delivers — which he cannot control and cannot withhold — are the book's most explicit statement of the divine commitment to Israel's future. The book's most powerful testimony to God's faithfulness comes from the mouth of a man who was paid to testify against it.

The travel itineraries embedded in Numbers — particularly the extended itinerary of chapter thirty-three, which lists forty-two stopping points in the wilderness journey — have sometimes been read as tedious historical record-keeping and skipped by readers looking for more theologically interesting content. They are, in fact, a form of witness: the careful enumeration of every place the community camped, every water source they found, every location where a crisis occurred or a death was recorded. The itinerary is the community's way of insisting that the wilderness years were not blank time. They were specific, located, historically real years in which specific things happened at specific places, and the record of those places is itself a form of testimony to the God who was present at every one of them.

The Nazarite vow of chapter six and its extension of the priestly holiness to any ordinary Israelite who chose it voluntarily reflects something important about the social world Numbers was written for: a community that took holiness seriously as a communal aspiration and not merely a priestly function. The Nazarite who abstained from wine, avoided contact with the dead, and maintained uncut hair for the duration of the vow was not performing an unusual religious eccentricity. They were embodying, in a temporary and voluntary form, the heightened consecration that the book's priestly legislation described as the permanent calling of the Aaronic priesthood. The provision for the Nazarite vow is Numbers' most direct statement that the holiness the covenant required was available beyond the boundaries of the priestly caste — that any member of the community, from any tribe, of any social standing, could choose a season of heightened consecration and receive from it the formation that sustained proximity to the holy God produces. The democratic impulse embedded in the Nazarite legislation is not a concession to popular religion. It is a formal expression of the conviction that the community's identity as a holy people belonged to the whole community and not only to the professionals who managed its worship infrastructure.

Preparing to Read Numbers Well

Understanding the community Numbers was written for, the structure that organizes its four movements from Sinai to the plains of Moab, the portrait of Moses it develops with unusual honesty, the theological significance of the wilderness as the space between promise and fulfillment, and the literary diversity that reflects the range of the wilderness experience: all of these are forms of orientation that prepare the reader to engage the text more fully.

But orientation is preparation, not replacement. The goal of everything this chapter has described is to position the reader to encounter Numbers directly — to receive its account of complaint and rebellion and divine response not as a remote historical record of ancient failures but as the searching, self-implicating narrative it is designed to be. Numbers was not written to make the reader feel superior to the Israelites who failed in the wilderness. It was written to press the question that their failure generates on every subsequent generation that reads their story: would you have done differently? And if not, what does the God who remained faithful to those who failed have to say to you in the wilderness you are currently navigating?

One final orientation point before entering the narrative directly: Numbers is best read in community rather than in isolation, precisely because the wilderness experience it describes is inherently communal rather than individual. The complaints in Numbers are collective. The failure at Kadesh Barnea is collective. The wandering is collective. The formation is collective. The second generation that enters the land is a community, not a collection of individuals who each privately decided to trust God at their own thresholds. Reading Numbers in a community context — in a small group or a congregation or a family that is willing to bring its own communal wilderness to the text together — surfaces dimensions of the book that individual reading misses entirely. The question of how the ten spies created fear in the community they reported to, and what Caleb and Joshua could have done differently to counter it, is not an interesting historical question when read in isolation. It is a live and pressing question about the dynamics of the specific community in which it is being read. Numbers was written for communities. It yields its deepest formation to communities that read it together and bring their shared wilderness honestly to the encounter.

Chapter 3

The World Behind the Book

"Then the LORD's anger burned against Israel and he made them wander in the wilderness forty years, until the whole generation of those who had done evil in his sight was gone."
--- Numbers 32:13

The Wilderness Terrain

The wilderness that Numbers describes is not a romantic metaphor. It is a specific, harsh, largely waterless landscape that presented real and constant threats to a large community on the move. The Sinai peninsula and the Negev desert through which Israel wandered are among the most inhospitable territories in the ancient Near East — rocky plateaus and sand plains where summer temperatures exceeded one hundred degrees, where water sources were scarce and unpredictable, where the terrain offered almost no shade and where the distance between one habitable location and the next could be measured in days of arduous travel. The complaints about food and water that run through Numbers are not the petulant expressions of a people ungrateful for miraculous provision. They are the responses of a community navigating conditions that genuinely threatened survival, and the miracles that address those complaints — the manna, the quail, the water from the rock — are genuine responses to genuine need.

Understanding the physical reality of the wilderness is essential for reading Numbers honestly. The Israelites were not complaining from positions of comfort about the quality of a provision that fully met their needs. They were a large community — Numbers gives census figures in the hundreds of thousands, though the precise interpretation of those numbers is debated — moving through terrain that could barely sustain their passage, dependent on divine provision for the most basic requirements of survival, and doing so under the leadership of a man whose authority was contested and whose access to the divine will was mediated through a tabernacle that had to be dismantled, transported, and reassembled at every stopping point. The logistics alone were staggering. The spiritual demands were greater still.

The specific geography of the wilderness journey in Numbers traces a route that archaeologists and biblical geographers have long attempted to reconstruct with precision. The community moved from Sinai northward through the wilderness of Paran, reached Kadesh Barnea in the wilderness of Zin where the catastrophic decision was made, and then spent the forty years wandering through the territories of the Sinai peninsula, the Negev, and the Transjordanian plateau before arriving at the plains of Moab east of the Jordan. The specific stopping points catalogued in Numbers thirty-three represent real locations, some of which have been tentatively identified with modern sites and some of which remain unknown. The geographic specificity of the wilderness narrative is not decorative detail. It is the insistence that these events happened in a real place, to real people, in conditions that shaped every aspect of the community's experience.

The Ancient Near Eastern World of the Late Bronze Age

The events Numbers describes are traditionally dated to the late Bronze Age — roughly the thirteenth century BCE, the period of Egyptian dominance over Canaan and the surrounding regions.

This was a world in which the great powers of Egypt, the Hittites, and the emerging Mesopotamian empires competed for control of the trade routes and agricultural resources of the Levant. The land of Canaan, toward which Israel was moving, was not empty territory waiting to be occupied. It was a mosaic of city-states, tribal territories, and agricultural communities embedded in the political and economic networks of the late Bronze Age world — a world whose structures were beginning to experience the stress that would produce the widespread collapse of Bronze Age civilization at the end of the thirteenth century.

Israel's movement through the Transjordanian territories — the lands east of the Jordan river that Numbers describes in its final sections — took place within this complex political landscape. The encounters with Sihon king of the Amorites and Og king of Bashan, the negotiations with Edom and the conflict with Midian, the Balaam narrative involving the Moabite king Balak — all of these are embedded in the specific political and ethnic geography of the late Bronze Age Levant. Understanding this context does not reduce the theological significance of these events, but it does prevent the misreading that treats them as taking place in a vacuum rather than within a specific historical world whose geography, politics, and ethnic relationships shaped every encounter the book describes.

The Military Organization of a Tribal People

The census that opens Numbers is not primarily a demographic exercise. It is a military census — a count of the men able to serve in Israel's army, organized by tribe, conducted in preparation for the military campaign that the entry into Canaan would require. The numbers recorded — over six hundred thousand fighting men, implying a total community of two million or more — have generated substantial scholarly debate about whether they are to be understood literally, symbolically, or as reflecting a different ancient numerical convention. Whatever their precise interpretation, the census reflects a community organized for war, not for wilderness wandering.

The arrangement of the camp described in chapters two and three extends this military logic into every dimension of the community's organization. The twelve tribes are arranged around the tabernacle in a specific order, with the Levites forming the innermost ring of the camp and the fighting men arranged by tribe in the outer rings. The marching order for the journey — which tribe goes first, which second, which carries what — is specified with the same precision. This is not simply religious ritual. It is the organization of a community that expects to fight for the territory it has been promised, and the precision of the arrangement reflects the conviction that the God who has called Israel to the land has also called Israel to take it by force if necessary.

The tension between this military preparedness and the actual wilderness experience is one of the most poignant features of Numbers. The community that was organized at Sinai for conquest spent forty years wandering instead, because the generation that was counted and organized at the beginning of the book was the generation that refused to use what it had been given. The second census at the end of the book counts a new generation — equally organized, equally prepared — standing on the threshold that their parents refused to cross.

The Canaanite Religious Landscape

The land Israel was moving toward was not religiously neutral territory. Canaan in the late Bronze Age was a world saturated with the worship of Baal and Asherah and a pantheon of local deities whose cults were embedded in the agricultural and urban landscape of the region. The high places, the sacred groves, the fertility rituals that organized the Canaanite religious calendar — all of these represented a coherent alternative to the covenant faith that Israel had received at Sinai, an alternative whose appeal to a community that had spent forty years in the wilderness would be significant and whose seductive power Numbers itself demonstrates in the episode at Baal Peor.

The Baal Peor incident of chapter twenty-five — in which Israel becomes sexually involved with Moabite women and begins worshipping their gods, provoking a divine plague that kills twenty-four thousand people — is the book's most concentrated demonstration of the danger the Canaanite religious landscape posed. It comes immediately after the Balaam narrative, in which God preserved Israel from the curse of a foreign prophet, and the juxtaposition is deliberate: the threat that Balak could not accomplish through hired divination, Israel accomplished through its own moral failure. The enemy that could not destroy Israel from the outside found a way in through the community's own choices.

The Canaanite religious world was deeply integrated into the agricultural rhythms that the land of Canaan's new inhabitants would need to understand and participate in. The timing of planting and harvest, the management of water resources, the fertility of flocks and herds — all of these were understood in the Canaanite religious framework as dependent on the favor of Baal and the local deities whose jurisdiction covered the specific territories in which the community was farming. The appeal of Canaanite religion to an agricultural people was therefore not primarily intellectual or theological. It was practical: these were the deities that the land's current inhabitants understood to be responsible for the land's productivity, and adopting their worship was the most straightforward way to secure the agricultural success that survival required. Numbers's account of Israel's repeated attraction to the worship of Canaanite deities is not a record of inexplicable apostasy. It is the honest documentation of a predictable human response to practical agricultural pressure in a new and unfamiliar land.

The World of Ancient Divination and Prophecy

The Balaam narrative of chapters twenty-two through twenty-four is one of the most revealing windows in the entire Hebrew Bible onto the world of ancient Near Eastern divination and prophecy. Balaam is presented not as a charlatan or a fraud but as a genuine practitioner of the divinatory arts — a man whose reputation for effective cursing and blessing was real enough that the Moabite king Balak sent a delegation from a considerable distance to hire him. The fees he was offered were substantial, the negotiations were extended, and the repeated divine interventions that frustrated his mission were required precisely because his abilities were genuine enough to pose a real threat.

The ancient Near Eastern world was one in which curses and blessings were understood to have real power — in which the spoken word of a recognized practitioner could affect the outcomes of battles, the fertility of fields, and the fates of communities in ways that the surrounding peoples took entirely seriously. Balaam operated within this world, and his reputation within it gave the Balaam narrative its stakes. The theological argument of the narrative is precisely that the God of Israel is not subject to the manipulations that ancient Near Eastern divination assumed were available to those with sufficient skill and sufficient payment. No amount of skill and no size of payment could compel the God of Israel to curse what he had blessed.

The talking donkey episode that precedes the oracles is the narrative's most memorable feature and its most theologically concentrated moment. The animal that Balaam is riding to deliver a curse against Israel sees the angel of the LORD blocking the path before her rider does, and when she stops, he beats her. The reversal — the beast seeing what the prophet cannot, the animal rebuking the man hired to speak divine words — is both comic and devastating. The one whose gift is supposed to be access to the divine is blind to a divine messenger that his donkey can see clearly. Numbers uses the episode to undercut any pretension to prophetic authority that rests on personal ability rather than genuine divine calling.

The Social World of a Community Under Stress

Numbers describes the social dynamics of a large community navigating extreme stress, and its portraits of those dynamics are among the most psychologically accurate in ancient literature. The complaints that run through the book are not the expressions of individual discontent but the social phenomena of a community whose collective anxiety has reached the point where it expresses itself as organized grievance. The pattern is consistent: a hardship arises, the community complains collectively, the complaint reaches Moses, Moses brings it to God, God responds — sometimes with provision, sometimes with judgment, and occasionally with both simultaneously.

The Korah rebellion of chapter sixteen is the most socially complex episode in Numbers and the one that most clearly reveals the dynamics of leadership challenge in a community under stress. Korah and his allies do not simply dispute Moses's decisions. They challenge the entire framework of his authority, using the language of democratic equality — the whole community is holy, every one of them — to undermine the specific structure of priestly and prophetic leadership that the Sinai covenant established. The challenge sounds reasonable on its surface, and it is presented sympathetically enough that the reader must work to understand why it is wrong. The issue is not whether the community is holy. It is whether the specific order of holiness that God established can be rearranged by human preference without consequence. The earth opening and swallowing Korah and his followers is the book's most dramatic answer to that question.

The social world of the wilderness camp was also a world of sustained proximity without the normal structures that proximity in settled life provides. The twelve tribes lived in close quarters, navigated shared resources, managed competing claims on leadership attention, and processed collective grief at the repeated deaths that the wilderness years required. Numbers records several moments of communal mourning — the deaths of Miriam and Aaron in particular — that give the wilderness narrative its human texture. The forty years were not only a period of complaint and rebellion. They were a period of births and deaths and ordinary community life, conducted under extraordinary conditions, in the company of a God whose presence was constant and whose purposes were not always immediately intelligible to those living inside them.

A World Defined by the Gap Between Promise and Reality

The world behind Numbers is finally a world organized around one of the most persistent features of covenant existence: the gap between what God has promised and what the present moment delivers. Israel in Numbers lived within this gap every day of the forty years the book describes. The promise was real — they had received it from the God who had already demonstrated his power to keep it, through the plagues, the exodus, the sea crossing, the provision in the wilderness. The present reality was also real — the wilderness was genuinely harsh, the journey was genuinely arduous, and the distance between the promise and its fulfillment was measured in years of grinding, repetitive, difficult daily existence.

The temptation to resolve this gap by abandoning the promise — by returning to Egypt, by worshipping the gods of the surrounding peoples, by replacing the leadership that was moving toward the promise with leadership that would accept a more manageable present — is the temptation that Numbers traces across its thirty-six chapters with unusual honesty. And the divine response to each iteration of that temptation is equally honest: the consequences of abandoning the promise are real, the judgment for doing so is genuine, and the faithfulness of the God who made the promise persists through both. Numbers does not minimize the gap between promise and reality. It insists on inhabiting it honestly, with full attention to both the difficulty of the present and the certainty of the future that the God of the promise has staked his own character on delivering.

The world behind Numbers is also the world of a community learning, for the first time in its history, what it means to be governed by law rather than by the direct, immediate experience of divine intervention. The exodus generation had experienced God's power in dramatic and unmistakable forms. They had seen the plagues. They had crossed the sea. They had stood at the foot of a burning mountain and heard the divine voice. The wilderness generation that followed them received that account as testimony rather than as lived experience, and their relationship to the God of the testimony was necessarily mediated by the legal and cultic structures that the Torah was establishing. Numbers is the first sustained account of what a covenant community governed by law looks like in practice — not the idealized community of the Levitical legislation, but the actual community of complaint and rebellion and legal dispute and inheritance question and leadership challenge that the wilderness produced. The gap between the idealized community that the law describes and the actual community that numbers documents is itself one of the most important contributions the book makes to the tradition: the insistence that the gap exists, that it is real, that it has consequences, and that the God who gave the law has not abandoned the community that consistently falls short of it.

Chapter 4

The Story or Flow of the Book

"Not one of you will enter the land I swore with uplifted hand to make your home, except Caleb son of Jephunneh and Joshua son of Nun."
--- Numbers 14:30

The Shape of Numbers

Numbers unfolds as the most emotionally difficult movement in the Torah's larger story — the record of what happened between the mountain of God's self-revelation and the land of God's promised gift, when the people who had been given everything they needed to receive that gift discovered that they could not trust the God who was offering it. The book is shaped by this failure in every dimension of its structure. It begins with the organized expectation of a community about to complete its journey. It ends with a new community standing where the first should have stood, inheriting the threshold that their parents refused to cross. Between these two census-marked moments is the long, painful, honest account of forty years that should not have been necessary.

Reading Numbers as a continuous narrative rather than as a collection of episodes requires following the emotional and theological arc of the whole — the gradual accumulation of complaint and rebellion and divine response that produces the catastrophic decision at Kadesh Barnea, the long grinding of the wilderness years that follow it, and the quiet, deliberate preparation of the new generation that closes the book. Each section illuminates the others, and the meaning of the whole is only visible when all four movements have been followed to their conclusions.

Sinai: Preparation and Departure

The opening ten chapters of Numbers are organized and expectant in a way that no subsequent section of the book quite matches. The community has been at Sinai for nearly a year — since the events of Exodus nineteen — and the preparations for departure are now complete. The census of the fighting men establishes the military strength of the community. The arrangement of the camp around the tabernacle establishes the spatial theology that will organize the community's movement. The consecration of the Levites and the legislation governing their service establishes the priestly infrastructure that will maintain the covenant relationship on the road. The second Passover establishes the continuity of the community's identity across the transition from encampment to travel. And the silver trumpets that will be used to signal the movement of the camp establish the practical mechanisms by which the community will coordinate its departure.

The tone of these chapters is purposeful and ordered. The cloud of the divine presence is over the tabernacle. When it lifts, Israel moves. When it settles, Israel camps. The community's movement is entirely directed by the visible presence of the God who is going with them. Everything is in place. The journey is about to resume, and the promised land is within reach. The reader who has followed the Torah from Genesis through Leviticus reaches the departure from Sinai with a sense of imminent completion — the promise made to Abraham is on the verge of fulfillment, and the community that will fulfill it has been prepared, organized, equipped, and directed by the same God who made the promise.

The Nazarite law of chapter six and the priestly blessing of the same chapter are among the most theologically concentrated passages in this opening section. The Nazarite vow establishes the principle that any member of the community, regardless of tribe or social position, can voluntarily commit to a heightened level of holiness for a specified period — making the priestly consecration available, in a temporary and voluntary form, to anyone in the community who chooses it. The Aaronic blessing that concludes chapter six — the LORD bless you and keep you; the LORD make his face shine on you and be gracious to you; the LORD turn his face toward you and give you peace — is the most beloved prayer in the Torah, and its placement here, immediately before the departure from Sinai, is a formal expression of the divine intention toward the community it is about to release into the wilderness.

The Wilderness: Complaint, Rebellion, and Catastrophe

Chapter eleven shatters this expectation almost immediately. The community has barely left Sinai before the complaints begin. Fire from the LORD burns at the edges of the camp. The people grieve over the monotony of the manna and the memory of Egyptian food. Moses reaches the breaking point, telling God that the burden of leading this community is more than he can carry. God sends quail — so much quail that the community gags on it — and a plague breaks out among those who craved meat. The community is moving, but it is moving in a spirit entirely different from the organized expectation of the opening chapters. The complaints that begin in chapter eleven will not stop until the wilderness years are over.

The challenge to Moses's leadership by Miriam and Aaron in chapter twelve introduces the theme of internal resistance to the divinely appointed order that will reach its most dangerous expression in the Korah rebellion of chapter sixteen. Miriam and

Aaron question whether God has spoken only through Moses — whether Moses's unique prophetic authority is genuinely unique or whether they share it equally. God's response is definitive: Moses is in a category apart, speaking with God face to face rather than through vision or dream. Miriam's leprosy and seven-day exclusion from the camp is the immediate consequence, and the episode establishes the principle that the specific structure of leadership God has appointed is not available for renegotiation by those who find it inconvenient.

Chapters thirteen and fourteen are the theological center of the book and the hinge on which the entire narrative turns. Twelve spies are sent to scout the land of Canaan — one from each tribe, including Caleb from Judah and Joshua from Ephraim. They return with abundant evidence of the land's fertility and unanimous testimony about the strength of its current inhabitants. Ten of the twelve conclude that the obstacles are insurmountable. Two — Caleb and Joshua — conclude that the God who has brought Israel this far is capable of bringing them the rest of the way. The ten carry the community. The people weep, wish they had died in Egypt, and propose electing new leadership to take them back. And God's response is the most devastating judgment in the wilderness narrative: none of the adults who have refused to trust him will enter the land. They will wander in the wilderness until the last of them has died, one year of wandering for each day the spies spent in Canaan — forty years in total.

The chapters that follow trace the long consequence of this decision with relentless honesty. The Korah rebellion challenges Moses's authority and is crushed with spectacular divine intervention. Aaron's rod buds, blossoms, and produces almonds overnight, confirming his priestly appointment against all challengers. Miriam dies. Aaron dies. Moses himself is disqualified at Meribah when he strikes the rock in frustrated anger rather than speaking to it as commanded — and the consequence is announced immediately and without softening: he will see the promised land but will not enter it. The wilderness years are not simply a waiting period. They are a period of active dying, in which the generation that refused to trust God is gradually, inevitably replaced by the generation that will.

The bronze serpent episode of chapter twenty-one is one of the wilderness narrative's most theologically significant and most frequently misread moments. The people complain again about the food and water, and this time poisonous serpents appear among them, biting and killing many. When the community repents and Moses intercedes, God instructs him to make a bronze serpent and lift it up on a pole — and anyone bitten who looks at it will live. The episode is the wilderness narrative's most concentrated image of the grace available within the consequences of failure: the judgment is real, the bites are real, and the provision for healing is also real, available to anyone willing to look toward the remedy that God has provided. Jesus will later use this image in the Gospel of John to describe the nature of his own lifting up in crucifixion — a connection that gives the bronze serpent episode one of the most significant trajectories of any passage in Numbers.

The Balaam narrative of chapters twenty-two through twenty-four interrupts the wilderness account with an episode that takes place entirely outside Israel's camp. The Moabite king Balak hires the renowned diviner Balaam to curse Israel as it encamps on the plains of Moab. Three times Balak arranges the sacrifices and positions Balaam for the curse. Three times Balaam opens his mouth and a blessing comes out instead. A fourth oracle follows, unsolicited and more sweeping than the first three. The narrative is the book's most explicit testimony to the divine commitment to Israel's future — delivered, with bitter irony, through the mouth of a man who was paid to testify against it. Chapter twenty-five immediately follows with the Baal Peor disaster, in which Israel does to itself what Balak could not do from the outside.

The New Generation: Preparation and Transition

Chapter twenty-six opens with the second census — a count of the new generation that has grown up in the wilderness, the children and grandchildren of the Sinai community who are now standing on the plains of Moab east of the Jordan. The census is not simply administrative bookkeeping. It is a theological statement: the generation that refused to enter the land has been fully replaced. The community that stands before Moses at the end of Numbers is not the community that stood before him at the beginning. The consequences of the first generation's failure have been completely worked out, and a new beginning is possible.

The daughters of Zelophehad episode in chapter twenty-seven is one of the most legally significant passages in Numbers and one of the most theologically revealing. Zelophehad has died in the wilderness, leaving five daughters and no sons. Under the inheritance law as understood to that point, his daughters would receive nothing. They bring their case directly to Moses, who brings it to God, who rules in their favor and establishes the principle of female inheritance for cases where a man dies without sons. The episode is remarkable for the directness with which the daughters address the legal system, the openness with which Moses acknowledges the limits of his own authority, and the willingness with which God establishes new legal precedent in response to a specific case. The law is not static in Numbers. It develops in response to the actual situations the community encounters.

The commissioning of Joshua as Moses's successor in the same chapter closes the leadership transition that the wilderness years made necessary. Moses lays hands on Joshua before the whole community, investing him with authority for the task that Moses himself will not complete. The gesture is both the acknowledgment of Moses's disqualification and the affirmation

that the mission continues regardless. Moses will see the land
from the top of a mountain. Joshua will lead the community into
it. The promise is not defeated by the leader's failure. It simply
passes to the next person God has appointed to carry it.

The Meaning of the Whole

Reading Numbers from beginning to end — following the arc
from organized expectation at Sinai through the catastrophic
failure at Kadesh Barnea through forty years of wilderness
consequence to the new generation's preparation on the plains of
Moab — produces an understanding of the whole that no
engagement with individual episodes can replicate. The book is
not a collection of wilderness stories. It is a sustained theological
argument about the relationship between divine faithfulness and
human unfaithfulness, pressed across four decades and two
generations.

The argument has two movements that cannot be separated
without distorting both. The first is the honest, unflinching
account of what unbelief costs — not as a theoretical proposition
but as the recorded experience of a real community whose refusal
to trust God at a critical moment produced consequences that
shaped the next forty years of their corporate existence. The
second is the equally honest account of the divine faithfulness that
persisted through and beyond that consequence — the manna
that kept arriving, the cloud that kept moving, the promise that
kept being kept across a generation of deaths that the
community's failure made necessary. Numbers holds both of these
movements simultaneously, and the meaning of the whole
depends on receiving both without softening either. The God of
Numbers is the God who judges and who remains faithful; the
community of Numbers is the community that fails and is
sustained anyway; and the wilderness of Numbers is the
wilderness that every subsequent community of faith has

navigated in its own form — the long middle between the promise and its fulfillment, where the question of trust is asked and answered every ordinary day.

The specific episodes that Numbers chose to preserve alongside the larger narrative arc deserve attention as well, because the selection itself is a theological argument. The daughters of Zelophehad could have been omitted without disturbing the wilderness narrative. The Balaam oracles could have been summarized rather than quoted at length. The detailed itinerary of chapter thirty-three could have been replaced with a simple statement that the community traveled from Sinai to the plains of Moab. The fact that these specific episodes were preserved and given the space they occupy in the canonical form of the book is evidence of a community that had learned something specific from each of them that the larger narrative alone could not convey. The daughters of Zelophehad preserved the principle that the law develops in response to the actual situations the community encounters — that the God who gave the law is not bound by its previous applications when a new situation reveals that the previous applications were incomplete. The Balaam oracles preserved the testimony that the God of the promise is sovereign over the speech of those who would undermine it — that no practitioner of any rival religious system can compel him to curse what he has committed to bless. The itinerary preserved the insistence that the wilderness years were not blank time — that every stopping point was real, every death was counted, every location where the divine presence met the community's need was worth recording. These are not incidental details. They are the specific testimonies that the community most needed to carry with it into the settled life that the wilderness was preparing it for.

The arc from the first census to the second census is also the arc of an argument about divine providence that Numbers presses on every reader who follows it to its conclusion. The first census counted the generation that would die in the wilderness. The second census counted the generation that would enter the land. Between those two countings, forty years passed and an entire generation was replaced. The God who organized the first census and directed the community's movement toward the threshold that the counted generation refused is the same God who organized the second census and directed the next generation's movement toward the same threshold. The mission did not change. The destination did not change. The promise did not change. What changed was the generation that was positioned to receive it — and the change happened because the God whose faithfulness organized the first census was also the God whose faithfulness organized the consequences of the first generation's failure and the formation of the second generation through those consequences. Reading the arc from first census to second census is reading the arc of a divine providence that is more patient, more purposeful, and more committed to its ultimate end than any single generation's capacity for faithfulness can either secure or defeat.

Chapter 5

Key Themes

"The LORD is slow to anger, abounding in love and forgiving sin and rebellion."
--- Numbers 14:18

Divine Faithfulness and Human Unfaithfulness

No theme is more central to Numbers than the sustained tension between divine faithfulness and human unfaithfulness — the gap between what God committed himself to do and what Israel proved willing to trust him to do. This tension is not resolved in the book. It is inhabited across thirty-six chapters and forty years with unusual honesty, and the honesty is itself a theological claim: that the God of Israel remained committed to his promise through levels of community failure that would have justified abandonment, and that this persistence in faithfulness is not a sign of divine indifference to the failure but of a commitment to the community that runs deeper than the community's merit.

The tension appears in its sharpest form in the exchange between Moses and God after the catastrophic failure at Kadesh Barnea. God tells Moses that he will destroy the community and start fresh with Moses alone — that the faithless generation has finally exhausted the divine patience. Moses responds not by agreeing that Israel deserves destruction but by appealing to the character of God himself: if you destroy them, what will the nations say about you? The argument is not that Israel deserves mercy. It is that the destruction of Israel would compromise the testimony of the God who claimed them as his people. God relents — not because Moses outargued him but because Moses understood what God was actually committed to. The faithfulness that Numbers describes is not the faithfulness of a God who ignores Israel's failures. It is the faithfulness of a God who weathers them without abandoning the promise they threaten.

This twin-engine dynamic — human failure pressing against divine faithfulness and divine faithfulness persisting through human failure — is the theological claim that every subsequent generation of the covenant community has needed to receive and re-receive. Communities that emphasize only the faithfulness risk producing complacency — the assumption that failure has no real consequences because God will persist anyway. Communities that emphasize only the failure risk producing despair — the conviction that the accumulated failures of the community have finally exceeded the capacity of the covenant to sustain them. Numbers holds both realities simultaneously, and the meaning of the whole depends on receiving both without softening either.

The specific vocabulary Numbers uses to describe divine faithfulness is itself theologically significant. The LORD is slow to anger, abounding in love and forgiving sin and rebellion — this is the divine self-description that Moses appeals to in his intercession after Kadesh Barnea, drawn from the earlier Sinai theophany of Exodus thirty-four. The vocabulary is not vague spiritual encouragement. It is a specific description of how the God of the covenant manages the tension between his holiness, which requires that failure have consequences, and his love, which commits him to the community despite the failures that his holiness cannot ignore. Numbers demonstrates across forty years what that specific character looks like in sustained practice — and the demonstration is the most extended and most honest portrait of divine faithfulness under pressure that the Torah contains.

The Wilderness as Formation

The forty years of wilderness wandering in Numbers have traditionally been read as punishment — the just consequence of the community's refusal to trust God at Kadesh Barnea, the sentence served for a specific act of faithlessness. This reading is accurate as far as it goes. Numbers itself presents the wandering as a consequence of the community's failure, and it does not soften that presentation. But reading the wilderness years only as punishment misses an equally important dimension of what Numbers describes: the wilderness as the space in which the community is being formed for the life it has been called to.

The generation that died in the wilderness was the generation that had been formed by Egypt. Their instinct under pressure was to remember Egypt favorably, to wish for its predictable oppression over the unpredictable demands of covenant freedom, to organize their desires around the provisions that slavery had offered rather than the promises that liberation had made. The forty years of wilderness did not redeem this generation — they died in it. But the generation that grew up in the wilderness, under the cloud and the manna and the daily provision of a God whose presence was the only constant in their lives, was a generation formed by the covenant rather than by Egypt. They had never known the fleshpots. They had only known the manna. And the manna, for all its limitations, was the provision of the God who had promised to bring them home.

The wilderness as formation rather than merely punishment is a distinction with significant practical implications for communities navigating their own long middles. The suffering of the wilderness years was not wasted even for the generation that died there — the Levitical system was established, the legal framework was developed, the leadership structure was refined, and the community that emerged from forty years of wilderness was more coherently organized around the covenant than the community that had entered it. The formation was real even when its primary beneficiaries were the next generation rather than those who underwent it.

The specific practices that sustained the community through the wilderness years are themselves formative in the deepest sense. The daily gathering of manna — which could not be stored, which appeared fresh each morning, which required the community to trust that tomorrow's provision would arrive as reliably as today's — was a daily exercise in the specific kind of trust that the wilderness was designed to develop. The prohibition on gathering more than the day's portion was not an arbitrary restriction. It was the daily discipline of learning to depend on God for tomorrow rather than on one's own accumulation today. Forty years of this practice was forty years of formation in the specific virtue that Kadesh Barnea had revealed was absent — the willingness to trust the God of the promise for what had not yet arrived.

Complaint and Its Consequences

Numbers is the Bible's most sustained and most honest treatment of complaint — the specific form that unbelief takes when the community's accumulated frustration with the distance between promise and present reality expresses itself in organized grievance. The complaints in Numbers are not presented as illegitimate. The food situation is genuinely difficult. The water situation is genuinely dangerous. The leadership challenges are genuinely significant. Numbers does not require its readers to pretend that the wilderness was comfortable or that the Israelites had nothing to complain about.

What Numbers does require is the recognition that complaint, however justified by circumstance, has consequences when it is directed against the God who has already demonstrated his willingness and ability to provide. The specific thing that condemns the wilderness generation is not that they found the wilderness hard — it was hard — but that they interpreted its hardness as evidence that God had abandoned them or deceived them, rather than as the predictable difficulty of a journey that the

God who called them to it had already promised to sustain them through.

The New Testament's engagement with the Numbers wilderness narrative reflects this distinction with precision. Paul writes to the Corinthians that the wilderness events were written as warnings for those on whom the fulfillment of the ages has come — and the specific warnings he cites are not about hardship but about the responses to hardship: craving evil things, idolatry, sexual immorality, testing the Lord, grumbling. Grumbling — the specific word for the Numbers complaint — is listed alongside idolatry and sexual immorality as the kind of response to wilderness conditions that the community of faith must guard against. The warning is not that the wilderness will be easy. It is that the community's response to its difficulty determines whether the wilderness becomes formation or destruction.

The complaint narratives of Numbers also reveal something important about the relationship between memory and faith. The Israelites' longing for Egypt was organized around a selective memory — the fish and the leeks and the cucumbers, stripped of the slavery and the infanticide and the systematic degradation that the same Egypt also contained. Their memory of the past was organized by what they wished the past had been rather than by what it actually was, and this selective memory made the difficult present look worse by comparison with an imagined past that never existed in the form they were remembering. The formation that Numbers offers against this tendency is not the suppression of memory but its reorientation — toward the accurate memory of what Egypt actually was, toward the accurate memory of what the God who liberated them from Egypt has already done, and toward the confident expectation of what the same God has already committed himself to do.

Leadership Under Impossible Conditions

Moses in Numbers is the Bible's most fully developed portrait of leadership under genuinely impossible conditions, and the portrait is valuable precisely because it refuses to idealize its subject or simplify his situation. Moses leads a community that does not want to go where he is trying to take them, that challenges his authority from multiple directions simultaneously, that reaches the threshold of its most important achievement and turns back, and that continues to need his leadership across forty years of a wilderness that their own failure had made necessary. He did all of this at enormous personal cost, to the point of exhaustion, and he was ultimately disqualified by a single moment of failure at the very end of the journey.

The portrait is psychologically realistic in ways that ancient leadership narratives rarely are. Moses' prayer in chapter eleven — in which he tells God that the burden is too heavy and he cannot carry it alone — is not presented as a failure of faith but as the honest expression of a man at the genuine limit of his capacity. God's response is not rebuke but provision: seventy elders will share the burden of leadership, distributing the weight that has been crushing Moses alone. The episode is one of the most practically relevant passages in Numbers for anyone who has ever been in a leadership position that required more than any single person can provide.

Moses's disqualification at Meribah is the most theologically difficult episode in his portrait. He has led the community faithfully for decades. He has interceded for them repeatedly, sometimes saving them from consequences their own behavior deserved. He has borne the burden of their leadership at enormous personal cost. And then, in a single moment of frustrated anger — striking the rock rather than speaking to it as God commanded — he forfeits the one thing he most wanted. The severity of the consequence has troubled readers across the centuries, and Numbers does not explain it away. What it does show is the principle that runs throughout the book: the mission belongs to God, the leader serves it rather than owns it, and the terms on which leadership is exercised are given by the one who called the leader rather than by the leader's own sense of what the moment requires.

The Theology of the Second Chance

The second census and the second generation are the most hopeful dimensions of Numbers and the clearest expression of one of its most distinctive theological contributions: the God of the wilderness gives the community a second chance that the community's own failure made necessary. The generation that refused to enter the land has died. The sentence has been fully served. And the God who pronounced the sentence is the same God who now prepares the next generation to receive what their parents refused — who plans the distribution of the land, who establishes the legal precedents that will govern the community's life within it, who commissions the leadership that will carry the mission forward.

The second chance in Numbers is not a softening of the consequences of the first generation's failure. Those consequences were real and were fully experienced. It is rather the demonstration that the consequences of failure, however real, are not the final word about a community whose God is committed to keeping his promise regardless of what the community does with it. The promise made to Abraham was not conditioned on the faithfulness of Abraham's descendants. It was grounded in the character of the God who made it. And that God, having worked out the consequences of one generation's refusal, simply turns to the next and asks again: will you trust me to bring you in?

The Presence of God on the Move

A final key theme in Numbers is the mobile divine presence —
the cloud by day and the fire by night that moved with the
community through the wilderness, setting the direction and pace
of the journey, settling when Israel was to camp and lifting when
Israel was to move. The presence is not incidental to the story. It
is its organizing reality. Every movement in Numbers is a
movement of the divine presence accompanied by the community
it has claimed, and the community's relationship to that presence
— whether it trusts the direction the cloud is moving, whether it
follows when it lifts and camps when it settles — is the practical
form that faith takes in the wilderness.

The theology of divine presence in Numbers is more
concrete and more demanding than most contemporary accounts
of God's presence acknowledge. The cloud is visible. Its
movements are unambiguous. When it moves, there is no
question about which direction God is going or whether the time
has come to break camp. The failure of the wilderness generation
is not a failure of perception — they could see the cloud as clearly
as anyone. It is a failure of trust: the willingness to follow where
the cloud is leading even when the destination it is moving toward
is more frightening than the wilderness it is moving away from.
The Kadesh Barnea failure is the moment when the community
looked at where the cloud was going and decided it preferred the
wilderness. Numbers describes the forty-year consequence of that
preference with characteristic honesty.

The mobile sanctuary that accompanied Israel through the
wilderness is the physical expression of this theme of divine
presence on the move, and it deserves more attention than it
typically receives in discussions of Numbers. The tabernacle was
not simply a portable worship center. It was the dwelling place of
the divine presence — the specific location in the midst of the
camp where the holy God had chosen to make his home among

his people, and around which the entire organization of the camp and the entire logic of the community's movement was organized. Every time the community broke camp and moved, the tabernacle was dismantled and carried by the Levites at the center of the marching order. Every time the community camped, the tabernacle was reassembled at the center of the new encampment. The community's life literally revolved around the divine presence — not metaphorically, but spatially, organizationally, and practically. The daily experience of being a member of this community was the daily experience of living in proximity to the place where God had chosen to dwell, of organizing one's movements around the movements of that presence, and of receiving from it the direction and provision on which every dimension of the community's survival depended. This is the context within which the community's complaints about food and water must be understood: not as the complaints of people who had been abandoned by God, but as the complaints of people who were camping in the shadow of God's tabernacle and finding that proximity to the divine presence was not the same thing as the comfortable life they had been hoping for.

Chapter 6

Where People Get It Wrong

"Why did you bring us up out of Egypt to this terrible place? It has no grain or figs, grapevines or pomegranates. And there is no water to drink!"
--- Numbers 20:5

Treating the Wilderness Generation as Uniquely Wicked

The most common and most distancing misreading of Numbers treats the wilderness generation as a uniquely faithless people whose failures are exceptional rather than representative — as a community whose specific wickedness produced a specific divine response that does not generalize to other communities in other times. On this reading, the wilderness narrative is a historical account of an unusually bad group of people getting what they deserved, and the reader's relationship to the account is primarily one of observation rather than self-implication. We are not like them. We would have believed. We would not have complained about the manna, wished for Egypt, or refused to enter the land when Caleb and Joshua told us we could.

This reading is precisely what the New Testament's engagement with the Numbers narrative refuses. Paul's use of the wilderness generation in 1 Corinthians ten is addressed to a community that considered itself spiritually sophisticated — that had received the sacraments, that had experienced genuine spiritual gifts, that had every reason to regard itself as beyond the kind of failure the Israelites demonstrated. Paul uses the wilderness narrative to argue exactly the opposite: that the specific failures of the Israelites are the standing temptations of every community that has received genuine grace, and that receiving grace does not immunize a community against the complaints, the idolatries, and the testing of God that the wilderness generation demonstrated. The wilderness generation is not a warning about other people's failures. It is a mirror for recognizing one's own.

Reading the Complaints as Simple Ingratitude

A related misreading treats the Israelites' complaints in Numbers as simple ingratitude — as the unreasonable whining of a people who had been given miraculous provision and were too spiritually shallow to appreciate it. On this reading, the complaints are evidence of a basic character deficiency in the wilderness community, and the divine judgment that follows them is the natural response to people who had no excuse for complaining given what they had received.

This reading misses the genuine difficulty of the wilderness conditions that the complaints arise from and therefore misses the specific nature of the failure the complaints represent. The Israelites in Numbers were not complaining from positions of comfort about the quality of a provision that fully met their needs. They were a large community navigating genuinely harsh terrain, dependent on provision that was real but monotonous, under leadership that was contested and under conditions that offered no certainty about the future. The complaints are understandable as human responses to genuinely difficult circumstances. What they reveal is not simple ingratitude but the specific spiritual failure of interpreting ongoing difficulty as evidence of divine abandonment rather than divine testing.

Receiving the complaints honestly — as the understandable but genuinely dangerous responses to wilderness conditions that they are — allows the reader to locate the actual failure precisely.

The failure is not that the wilderness was hard. It is that hardness was interpreted as betrayal. And recognizing the specific location of the failure makes the warning of Numbers genuinely applicable rather than merely historical: the question for every subsequent community navigating its own wilderness is not whether the conditions are difficult but whether the difficulty is being interpreted as abandonment or as the predictable challenge of a journey the God who called them to it has already promised to sustain them through.

Misreading Balaam as a Simple Villain

The character of Balaam in Numbers has generated centuries of interpretive controversy, and one of the most persistent misreadings treats him as a straightforward villain — a wicked man who tried to curse Israel for money and was thwarted by God. This reading is supported by later biblical references to Balaam that associate him with Israel's sin at Baal Peor and describe him as a negative example. But it misses the complexity of Balaam as Numbers itself presents him and therefore misses the theological argument the Balaam narrative is making.

Numbers presents Balaam as a genuine practitioner of the divinatory arts whose abilities were real enough to be worth hiring at considerable expense. It also presents him as genuinely responsive to the divine will — he refuses to go with Balak's first delegation when God tells him not to, he seeks divine guidance repeatedly before each oracle, and when the oracles come out as blessings rather than curses, the narrative presents this not as Balaam deceiving Balak but as Balaam speaking what he has genuinely received. The theological argument of the Balaam narrative is lost if Balaam is reduced to a simple villain. The argument is that the God of Israel is sovereign over the words of those who speak in the name of the divine — that no amount of skill, no size of payment, and no sophistication of divinatory technique can compel the God of Israel to curse what he has committed himself to bless.

The later biblical tradition's negative assessment of Balaam — which identifies him with the counsel that led Israel into the Baal Peor disaster — adds a dimension to his character that Numbers itself only hints at in the final verses of chapter twenty-four. The Balaam of Numbers is a more complex figure than the villain of later tradition: a genuine prophet who could not control the blessings that came through him, but who apparently found other ways to serve the interests of those who hired him. The complexity is not a literary inconsistency. It is an honest portrait of a figure whose gifts and whose allegiances pulled in different directions, and who ultimately serves the narrative's theological argument in both his blessing and his failure.

Treating Moses's Disqualification as Disproportionate

The episode at Meribah in which Moses strikes the rock rather than speaking to it, and the consequence — that he will see the promised land but not enter it — has troubled readers across the centuries and generated a persistent misreading that treats the punishment as disproportionate to the offense. Moses has led the community faithfully for decades. He has interceded for them repeatedly, sometimes at great personal cost. He has borne the weight of their leadership under conditions that were genuinely impossible. And for one act of frustrated anger, he is barred from the destination he has been moving toward his entire adult life. This seems, to many readers, unfair.

The misreading arises from evaluating Moses's disqualification by the logic of proportional punishment rather than by the logic of representative leadership that Numbers is actually applying. Moses's specific failure at Meribah was not simply striking a rock instead of speaking to it. It was speaking to the community in a way that implied the water was produced by his own power — listen, you rebels, must we bring you water out of this rock? — rather than by the power of the God he was supposed to be representing. For an ordinary Israelite, this failure would be significant. For the leader whose specific calling was to represent the divine character to the community, it was disqualifying, because it corrupted precisely the function the leader existed to perform.

The disqualification of Moses is not a disproportionate punishment for a minor offense. It is the consistent application of the principle that runs through the entire book: the closer one stands to the holy God in a representative capacity, the more completely one's actions must correspond to the character of the one being represented. The principle is not unique to Moses. It is the same principle that cost Nadab and Abihu their lives in Leviticus for unauthorized fire at the altar — unauthorized approach to the holy by those whose specific function was to mediate access to it. Moses's consequence is different in form from Nadab and Abihu's because his failure is different in character. But the underlying principle is identical, and recognizing that principle removes the apparent disproportionality from the Meribah account entirely.

Reducing the Wilderness Years to Punishment Only

As noted in Chapter 5, one of the most persistent misreadings of Numbers treats the wilderness years exclusively as punishment — the just consequence of the community's failure at Kadesh Barnea, the forty-year sentence served for a specific act of faithlessness. This reading is accurate but incomplete, and its incompleteness produces a distorted account of what the wilderness years were for and what they accomplished.

The forty years were a consequence, and Numbers never softens that fact. But they were also the period in which the new generation was formed — in which the community was organized, its legal framework developed, its leadership structure refined, its priestly institution established, and its identity as the people of God embedded in practices and structures that would sustain it through the conquest and settlement that followed. The wilderness years were not wasted time. They were formation time, and the community that emerged from them was more coherently organized around the covenant than the community that entered the wilderness had been. Reading the wilderness years only as punishment misses the formative dimension that Numbers consistently displays alongside the punitive one.

Misreading the Korah Rebellion as Legitimate Protest

The Korah rebellion of chapter sixteen is perhaps the most frequently misread episode in Numbers, and the misreading typically runs in one of two directions. The first treats Korah's challenge — all the community is holy, every one of them; why do you set yourself above the LORD's assembly? — as a legitimate democratic critique of Moses's autocratic leadership, and the divine destruction of Korah and his followers as evidence of a troubling divine preference for hierarchy over equality. The second treats the rebellion as straightforward wickedness and misses the theological sophistication of Korah's challenge.

Both misreadings miss the specific nature of what Numbers is diagnosing. Korah's claim that the whole community is holy is not wrong as a theological statement — Leviticus itself affirms that Israel is a kingdom of priests and a holy nation. What is wrong is the use of that true theological claim to dissolve the specific order of holiness that God established — in which not all members of the community have the same access to the sanctuary or the same responsibilities within it. The rebellion is not simply a power grab. It is a theologically sophisticated argument that gets the general principle right and applies it in a way that overrides the specific divine order. The earth opening to swallow Korah is not the suppression of legitimate protest. It is the demonstration that the specific order God established is not available for revision by the application of general principles, however correct those principles may be in the abstract.

Collapsing Numbers into a Morality Tale About Obedience

The most reductive misreading of Numbers treats the book as a morality tale in which the message is simple: obey God and things will go well; disobey God and things will go badly. On this reading, the wilderness narrative is organized entirely around the reward-and-punishment logic of behavioral compliance, and the lesson of the forty years is that Israel should have done what it was told.

This reading is not entirely wrong, but it is drastically insufficient. Numbers is not primarily a book about the importance of obedience. It is a book about the character of the God who commanded obedience and the character of the community that was commanded. The failure at Kadesh Barnea was not a failure of compliance with a specific divine instruction. It was a failure of trust in the God who gave the instruction — a failure to believe that the God who had already done everything he had promised to do up to that point was capable of doing the one remaining thing he was asking them to trust him for. The lesson of Numbers is not that obedience produces good outcomes, though it does. The lesson is that trust in the character of the God who commands is the foundation on which obedience rests, and that when that trust collapses, compliance becomes impossible regardless of how much the community knows about what it is supposed to do. Israel at Kadesh Barnea knew exactly what God was asking. They simply could not believe he was capable of delivering it. That is the failure Numbers is diagnosing, and no morality tale about obedience gets close to naming it.

There is one further misreading worth naming briefly: the misreading that treats the legislative sections of Numbers — the laws governing Levitical service, the Nazarite vow, the procedures for handling various ritual situations, the inheritance regulations — as irrelevant filler between the more narratively interesting episodes. This misreading applies to Numbers the same logic that treats Leviticus as archaeology: since the specific laws are no longer operative, they have nothing to say to contemporary readers beyond their historical context. The corrective is the same corrective that applies to Leviticus: the theological logic that organizes the legislation is as operative as it has ever been, even when the specific mechanisms through which that logic is enacted have changed. The legislation of Numbers is organized around the conviction that the God who called this community to its destination cares about the specific, practical, organizational details of how the community moves toward it — that the sacred and the administrative are not two separate domains requiring separate frameworks, but one integrated life whose every dimension is accountable to the character of the God whose presence gives it its reason for existing. Communities that have learned to read their own administrative and organizational life as a dimension of their covenant faithfulness rather than as the necessary but spiritually neutral infrastructure of their religious work have received something from Numbers' legislative sections that the narrower focus on narrative alone cannot provide.

There is one more misreading worth naming before leaving this chapter: the misreading that treats Numbers as essentially negative — as the biblical book of failure, complaint, and judgment, whose primary contribution to the canon is the documentation of what not to do and the corresponding warnings about the consequences of doing it. On this reading, Numbers is a cautionary anthology whose value is primarily negative: useful for knowing what to avoid, but not a source of positive formation or genuine hope. This reading misses the book's most significant contribution. Numbers is not primarily a book about failure. It is primarily a book about the God who remained present and faithful through failure that would have justified departure. The failure is real and is documented honestly. But the manna that arrived every morning for forty years, the cloud that moved every day for forty years, the promise that was kept across every rebellion and every Kadesh Barnea and every Baal Peor that the wilderness produced — these are the primary testimony of Numbers, and they constitute the most sustained portrait of divine faithfulness under pressure available anywhere in the biblical canon. The misreading that reduces Numbers to a cautionary tale has extracted the warning from the witness and thrown the witness away. Numbers without its account of divine faithfulness is not Numbers. It is a selective anthology in service of a moralism that the book itself consistently transcends.

Chapter 7

What It Means for Modern Life

"If the LORD is pleased with us, he will lead us into that land."
--- Numbers 14:8

Navigating the Long Middle

The most direct practical contribution Numbers makes to modern
life is its sustained, honest engagement with the territory that most
communities of faith are actually occupying most of the time: the
long middle between a genuine promise and its fulfillment, the
stretch of ordinary days in which the destination is real but not yet
visible and the question of whether to keep moving toward it
presses itself on every member of the community in slightly
different form. Numbers is the biblical book that most completely
inhabits this territory, and its insights about what the long middle
does to communities and what communities must do in the long
middle are as applicable to the contemporary reader as they were
to the first communities that preserved the wilderness narrative.

The first practical implication of Numbers for modern
communities is the need to develop an honest vocabulary for the
wilderness experience — a way of naming what the long middle
actually feels like without either dramatizing it into crisis or
minimizing it into mere inconvenience. The Israelites in Numbers
named their experience loudly and collectively, and their naming
was honest even when their interpretation was wrong. What they
got wrong was not the acknowledgment that the wilderness was
hard but the conclusion that hardness meant abandonment.
Modern communities of faith navigating their own long middles

need both halves of this correction: the freedom to name the difficulty honestly, and the discipline to resist the interpretation that difficulty means the God who called them to the journey has lost interest in seeing it completed.

Developing this vocabulary requires communities to engage Numbers directly rather than rushing past its accounts of complaint and failure toward the more comfortable portions of the biblical narrative. The communities that have spent the most time in the wilderness narrative tend to develop the most realistic and most resilient faith — not because the narrative makes the wilderness easier but because it names the wilderness accurately and holds out the sustained divine faithfulness that persists through it as the ground on which genuine hope rests. Numbers does not promise that the long middle will be short. It promises that the God who is in it with the community is the God who has committed himself to bringing the community through.

Resisting the Pull Toward Egypt

The Israelites' persistent longing to return to Egypt is one of the most psychologically acute observations in Numbers, and its modern application is more direct and more personal than its ancient Near Eastern specificity might suggest. The Egypt that the Israelites longed for was not the real Egypt of slavery and oppression. It was the remembered Egypt of adequate provision and predictable conditions — the Egypt that the wilderness had transformed in memory into a bearable alternative to the uncertainty of the desert road. The longing was not for the reality of where they had been but for the imagined safety of the known, however painful the known had actually been.

Every community of faith navigating a difficult transition knows this longing in some form. The congregation that spent decades in a building that was too small and too expensive to maintain will discover, after moving to a better space, a subset of its members who remember the old building with an affection that bears no relationship to how they felt about it when they were in it. The organization that has been through a painful leadership transition will find members whose nostalgia for the previous leader grows in inverse proportion to their actual satisfaction during that leader's tenure. The individual who has made a costly decision to follow a calling they believed was genuine will discover, in the first months of difficulty, a longing for the life they left that makes the difficulty of the present seem larger than it is and the life before seem better than it was.

Numbers addresses this longing by naming it honestly and by showing its consequences without softening them. The community that organized its desires around the return to Egypt rather than the movement toward the promised land was the community that spent forty years dying in the wilderness. The practical application is not the suppression of the longing — it is real, and suppressing it produces dishonesty rather than faith — but the refusal to organize the community's movement around it. The question Numbers presses on every community navigating the pull toward Egypt is not whether the longing is present but whether the community is willing to keep moving in the direction of the promise rather than the direction of the remembered past.

Leading When the Community Cannot Believe

The portrait of Moses in Numbers has more to say to contemporary leaders than almost any other leadership portrait in Scripture, precisely because it refuses to idealize its subject or simplify his situation. Moses led a community that did not want to go where he was taking it, that challenged his authority from multiple directions simultaneously, that reached the threshold of its most important achievement and turned back, and that continued to need his leadership across forty years of a wilderness that their own failure had made necessary. He did all of this at enormous personal cost, to the point of exhaustion, and he was ultimately disqualified by a single moment of failure at the very end of the journey.

The practical wisdom of Moses's leadership portrait in Numbers is concentrated in several specific moments. The prayer of chapter eleven — in which he tells God that the burden is too heavy and he cannot carry it alone — and God's response of distributing the burden among seventy elders is the most direct practical instruction in the book about the sustainable organization of leadership. No single person is designed to bear what Moses was bearing alone. The distribution of leadership responsibility is not a concession to weakness. It is the recognition of a design feature of the human person that even the greatest leader cannot override indefinitely.

The commissioning of Joshua as Moses's successor is equally significant for contemporary leadership. Moses does not negotiate his disqualification or resist the transition. He lays hands on Joshua publicly, invests him with the authority the mission requires, and steps aside from the mission he has given his life to — knowing that he will see the destination from a distance but will not enter it. The capacity to transfer leadership gracefully, to prioritize the mission over the leader's own attachment to it, and to invest the next generation of leadership with the authority the mission requires rather than hoarding that authority to the end — this is the leadership wisdom that Numbers commends through Moses's example.

The specific challenge that Moses's portrait in Numbers presses on contemporary leaders is the challenge of leading people who doubt the destination the leader is trying to move them toward. Most leadership development focuses on vision casting and team alignment — on producing in the community the shared conviction that the destination is worth moving toward. Numbers is honest about what happens when this effort fails: the leader is left trying to move a community that has decided it prefers the wilderness to the threshold. Moses did not resolve this situation. He navigated it faithfully across forty years, absorbing the community's failure without abandoning his own calling, and was ultimately honored not by entering the land himself but by producing a community — through the formation of the wilderness years — that was capable of entering it under the leadership of his successor.

The Contagion of Collective Doubt

One of the most practically significant contributions Numbers makes to modern life is its unflinching account of how collective doubt spreads and what it costs. The ten spies who returned from Canaan with a discouraging report did not simply express their own fear. They created fear in those who heard them, and the fear they created was more powerful than the confidence that Caleb and Joshua tried to counter it with. The ten outvoted the two, and the community's collective failure of faith became the sentence that forty years of wilderness would fulfill. The dynamics of communal unbelief that Numbers describes are among the most psychologically accurate observations in ancient literature, and they apply to every community in every era with depressing consistency.

Collective doubt spreads through communities by the same mechanisms in every generation. The conversation in the camp that begins with one family's honest concern and ends with the whole community's paralysis. The influential voice that frames the obstacles in terms designed to produce despair rather than challenge. The cumulative weight of multiple negative perspectives that creates a mood of impossibility even when the factual situation does not warrant it. Numbers presents this dynamic with unusual clarity, and its presentation is a warning and a resource simultaneously: a warning about the real danger of allowing the perspectives of the most fearful to define the community's collective assessment of its situation, and a resource for understanding the mechanics of how that danger operates so that it can be recognized and countered.

The counter to collective doubt in Numbers is not optimism — the forced positive reframing of a situation that is genuinely difficult. It is the specific, grounded, historically anchored confidence of Caleb and Joshua: the land we passed through and explored is exceedingly good. If the LORD is pleased with us, he will lead us into that land. Do not rebel against the LORD. And do not be afraid of the people of the land, because we will devour them. Their protection is gone, but the LORD is with us. Caleb and Joshua do not deny that the land is inhabited by strong people. They do not pretend the obstacles are smaller than they are. They simply assess the situation from a different reference point — from the character of the God who has already done everything he promised to do, rather than from the size of the obstacles that remain.

Receiving Difficulty as Formation

The practical implication of the wilderness-as-formation theme is the most demanding and the most necessary contribution Numbers makes to communities navigating extended difficulty. The instinct of most communities under sustained pressure is to treat the difficulty as a problem to be solved or escaped rather than as a context in which something necessary is being produced. The community that has been in a long wilderness — a season of institutional difficulty, a period of numerical decline, a stretch of years in which the fruit it was expecting has not appeared — will almost inevitably be tempted to interpret the absence of the expected outcomes as evidence that something has gone wrong, that the calling was mistaken, or that the God who promised has not delivered.

Numbers offers a different interpretive framework. The wilderness years were not wasted years. The formation that happened in them — the organizational development, the legal refinement, the leadership transition, the identity consolidation that took place across forty years of wandering — was real formation that the promised land could not have produced on the same timeline. The community that entered Canaan under Joshua was a more coherently organized, more legally sophisticated, more self-consciously covenantal community than the community that left Egypt under Moses, and the wilderness years were the context in which that development took place. The formation was real even though the people who underwent it mostly did not enter the promised land.

This framework has specific and practical implications for communities in extended difficulty. The question it generates is not whether the difficulty is real — it is — but what is being produced in the community through the difficulty that could not be produced any other way. The congregation that has spent years navigating a painful institutional crisis may find, on the other side of it, that it knows things about its own identity, its actual commitments, and the character of its God that it could not have known without the crisis. The individual who has spent years in a wilderness of unfulfilled promise may find, when the promise finally arrives, that they are capable of receiving it and stewarding it in ways that their pre-wilderness self was not. Numbers does not promise that the difficulty will be short. It insists that the difficulty is not empty.

The Promise That Persists Through Failure

The most sustaining and most theologically significant practical contribution of Numbers is the one embedded in its overall narrative arc: the promise persists through failure. The generation that refused to trust God at Kadesh Barnea died in the wilderness.

The consequences of their failure were real and were fully experienced. And on the other side of those consequences, the God who had made the promise to Abraham stood on the plains of Moab with a new generation and prepared them to receive what their parents had refused.

This is the practical word that Numbers speaks most directly to communities carrying the weight of their own accumulated failures. Not the word that failure has no consequences — it does, and Numbers documents them honestly across forty chapters. But the word that the consequences of failure, however real, are not the final word about a community whose God has committed himself to keeping a promise that he did not make because the community deserved it. The promise was made because of who God is, not because of who Israel was. And the God who made it on that basis is the God who keeps it on that basis — through the failure and beyond it, working out the consequences that faithlessness requires while simultaneously preparing the next generation to receive what the previous one refused.

For modern communities of faith navigating their own histories of failure — the accumulated institutional compromises, the leadership failures, the seasons of unfaithfulness that produced consequences still being worked through — Numbers offers the most honest and the most grounded hope available. Not the hope that the past did not happen or that its consequences have been wished away, but the hope of a God whose commitment to his people is grounded in his own character rather than in their merit, and who has demonstrated across the entire wilderness narrative that he is capable of keeping his promise through conditions that would have justified abandonment at any point along the way. The promise persists. That is what Numbers most needs its readers to know.

The practical movement from receiving these contributions of Numbers to embodying them in the life of a community requires one additional element that the book itself models: the willingness to name the specific wilderness one is in with the same specificity that Numbers names the Israelites' wilderness. Vague acknowledgment that life is hard and the journey is long does not engage Numbers honestly. Numbers is a specific book about specific people in a specific terrain facing specific hardships at specific locations named in specific itineraries. The community that engages Numbers with equivalent specificity — naming the specific provision that feels inadequate, the specific threshold it is refusing to cross, the specific Caleb voices it is failing to listen to, the specific Egypt it is longing to return to — is the community that Numbers can form most deeply. The formation that Numbers produces is not the formation of the community that has appreciated its general message. It is the formation of the community that has allowed its specific message to press on the specific conditions of its specific wilderness with the specificity that both the book and the wilderness deserve.

Chapter 8

Modern Reflection

"My servant Caleb has a different spirit and follows me
wholeheartedly."
--- Numbers 14:24

What Numbers Does to the Reader Over Time

The previous chapter examined what Numbers makes possible for modern readers — how its specific accounts of wilderness complaint, leadership exhaustion, communal doubt, and divine faithfulness can function as practical resources for communities navigating their own long middles. This chapter is concerned with a different and slower question: what Numbers does to the reader who returns to it across different seasons of life. Not the immediate application of a passage to a specific situation, but the formation that happens when a person or a community engages the wilderness narrative seriously and repeatedly, bringing each season's specific experience to the text and allowing the text to press its claims toward that experience with the depth that sustained engagement produces.

Numbers is not designed to yield its full significance in a single reading. Its formation is cumulative — dependent on the reader bringing to it, across multiple engagements, the increasingly specific experience of what the wilderness actually costs and what the divine faithfulness that persists through it actually looks like from the inside. The reader who first encounters the wilderness generation in their twenties, from a position of relative comfort and limited wilderness experience, will find the community's failure baffling and their complaints ungenerous. The reader who returns to the same narrative in their forties, from the inside of a genuine long middle that has gone on longer than expected and produced less than was hoped, will find the complaints not baffling but entirely recognizable — and the divine faithfulness that persists through them not obvious but genuinely remarkable.

The Distinctive Character of Numbers' Encounter

Numbers engages the reader with an honesty about community failure that is unusual in sacred literature and that becomes more rather than less valuable the more honestly the reader brings their own community's experience to the encounter. Most religious literature presents the community of faith in idealized or aspirational form — describing what the community should be rather than what it consistently is. Numbers does neither. It describes what the community actually was, across forty years of documented failure, with the kind of specificity and the kind of unflinching attention to the gap between calling and performance that produces self-recognition rather than self-congratulation in the reader who approaches it honestly.

The complaint narratives of Numbers are the most distinctive feature of this honesty. The Israelites' complaints are recorded with enough specificity — the memory of Egyptian food, the boredom of the manna, the fear of the Canaanite cities, the wish to have died in Egypt — that the reader who has navigated their own version of the long middle will find them not distant and historical but uncomfortably contemporary. The specific form that the Israelites' failure took is less important than the underlying dynamic it represents: the community that interprets ongoing difficulty as divine abandonment rather than divine testing, that organizes its desires around the return to what was known rather than the movement toward what has been promised. Every community of faith has inhabited that dynamic in some form, and the reader who engages Numbers with enough honesty to recognize it will find the text pressing on their own community's specific version of it with uncomfortable precision.

The Complaint Narratives as Formation

The complaint narratives of Numbers produce their most significant formation not in readers who observe the Israelites' failures from a comfortable distance but in readers who bring their own complaints honestly to the text and allow the text's diagnosis to press on those complaints. The formation this requires is the opposite of the self-protective distance that the moralistic reading of Numbers tends to produce — the reading that uses the Israelites' failures as confirmation of the reader's own spiritual superiority rather than as a mirror for recognizing the reader's own version of the same failure.

Bringing one's own complaints to Numbers honestly means acknowledging the specific forms that the interpretation of difficulty as abandonment takes in one's own experience — the prayers that feel unanswered for long enough that the silence begins to feel like absence rather than timing, the promises that were genuinely received and genuinely believed and have not yet been fulfilled in the form or on the timeline that was expected, the community's sustained difficulty that has begun to produce in its members the same collective erosion of trust that the manna produced in the Israelites. None of these are admissions of exceptional spiritual failure. They are the honest acknowledgment of what the long middle does to ordinary faith in ordinary communities, and the acknowledgment is the precondition for receiving what Numbers has to say about it.

The formation that honest engagement with the complaint narratives produces across multiple readings is a realistic and resilient faith — not the faith that the wilderness will be short or that the difficulty will resolve quickly, but the faith that has looked at the longest and most painful wilderness narrative in the Torah and found in it not the absence of divine faithfulness but its most sustained and most searching demonstration. The Israelites complained for forty years. The manna arrived every morning for forty years. Both are equally true, and the reader who has received both truths fully has a more durable foundation for wilderness faith than any amount of comfort and encouragement can produce.

The Balaam Oracles and Being Seen by God

The Balaam oracles of chapters twenty-two through twenty-four have a specific formative function that is easy to miss if they are read primarily as evidence of God's sovereignty over foreign divination. They are also — and perhaps primarily — the moment in Numbers when the community of Israel hears itself described by someone who had every incentive to describe it otherwise. Balaam was hired to curse Israel. What comes out of his mouth instead is a portrait of the community from the outside, from the perspective of one who cannot control what he says, that is more generous and more hopeful than anything the community was saying about itself in the preceding chapters.

The community that has spent the preceding narrative complaining about its food, wishing it were back in Egypt, and deciding that the God who has brought it this far cannot bring it the rest of the way, suddenly finds itself described as a people who have been blessed by God, who are camped in security under divine protection, who are destined for greatness that the surrounding nations would do well to notice. The community does not hear the oracles directly in the narrative — they are delivered to Balak on a hilltop while Israel sleeps in its tents below. But the reader who holds both the complaint narratives and the Balaam oracles simultaneously has access to the gap between how the wilderness generation understood itself and how the God it was doubting understood it.

The formation this gap produces across sustained reading is the gradual recognition that the community's self-assessment in the wilderness is not the only assessment available — that the God who is being doubted is also the God who is blessing what is being doubted, who sees potential in what sees only failure in itself, and who speaks that potential through channels the community cannot control and in contexts the community cannot observe. The Balaam oracles are Numbers' most unexpected gift to the reader navigating their own wilderness: the reminder that the God who appears silent from inside the long middle may be speaking about the community on hilltops it cannot see.

Kadesh Barnea and the Formation of Honest Self-Examination

The Kadesh Barnea account — the catastrophic refusal to enter the land when it was within reach — is the passage in Numbers that produces the most searching formation in the reader who brings to it the honest question: would I have done differently? The formation requires resisting the comfortable assumption that the answer is yes — that one would have been Caleb rather than one of the ten, that one's own faith is more robust than the wilderness generation's, that the failure at Kadesh Barnea represents an exceptional level of faithlessness that one's own community would not reproduce.

The honest engagement with Kadesh Barnea across different seasons of reading produces a progressively more realistic answer to that question. The reader who has navigated their own version of the threshold — the moment when the promised destination was within reach and the obstacles between the present position and the destination looked larger than the God who promised had accounted for — will recognize in the Israelites' response not an exceptional failure but a familiar one. The ten spies were not unusually faithless people. They were ordinary people making an ordinary human assessment of an extraordinary situation — one in which the evidence of the obstacles was visible and immediate while the evidence of the God who had overcome every previous obstacle was historical and remembered.

The Second Generation as the Shape of Sustained Reading

The second generation of Numbers — the community that grew up in the wilderness, that has never known Egypt, that stands on the plains of Moab ready to receive what their parents refused — is the image of what sustained engagement with the wilderness narrative produces in those who receive it honestly across multiple seasons of reading. The second generation has not failed to enter the land. They were not at Kadesh Barnea. They have inherited a wilderness they did not earn and a promise they did not experience firsthand, and they are now being prepared to receive what the promise contains.

This is the position of every reader who engages Numbers from the outside — who was not in the wilderness, who did not eat the manna, who did not experience the divine presence in the cloud and the fire, but who has inherited the account and who is now being prepared by that account for a reception of the promise that will take the form appropriate to their own time and circumstances. The second generation received the promise through the account of what the first generation had experienced and failed. Every subsequent reader receives it the same way. And the formation that sustained engagement with that account produces is the formation of the second generation: not the naivety of those who have never failed, but the readiness of those who know exactly what failure costs and what the God who outlasts failure is capable of doing with a community willing to trust him at the threshold.

The Promise of Divine Companionship on the Journey

The most sustaining formation that Numbers produces across repeated engagement is not a theological proposition about divine faithfulness but a developed sense of the specific character of the God who demonstrated that faithfulness across forty years of wilderness. The God of Numbers is the God who stayed — who did not abandon the community when it wished for Egypt, did not revoke the manna when the community complained about it, did not withdraw the cloud when the community refused to follow it to Kadesh Barnea, did not destroy the community when Moses interceded for it, and did not allow the consequences of one generation's failure to terminate the promise that the failure was unable to defeat.

This is the portrait of God that extended engagement with Numbers produces — not the abstract theological proposition that God is faithful, but the specific, tested, wilderness-proven knowledge of what divine faithfulness looks like from inside the long middle when the manna has been arriving every morning for forty years and the destination is still not in sight. The reader who has spent serious time in Numbers has a more durable foundation for faith in the long middle than any amount of encouragement or exhortation can provide, because they have seen what the God they are trusting did across forty years with a community far less faithful than they are. The wilderness is long. The manna arrives every morning. The promise is kept. This is what Numbers, read carefully and returned to honestly, has always been designed to produce.

The formation that sustained engagement with Numbers produces is also, characteristically, a communal formation rather than an individual one. The reader who engages Numbers alone, in the privacy of their own spiritual life, will find it pressing with some force. The community that engages Numbers together — that brings its collective wilderness to the text, that names its collective complaints alongside the Israelites' complaints, that asks together the Kadesh Barnea question about the threshold it is collectively facing — will find it pressing with a force that individual engagement cannot replicate. The wilderness generation failed collectively. The formation the wilderness produced was collective. The second generation received the promise collectively. Numbers was written for a community, and its deepest formation happens in community. The community that reads Numbers together across seasons of shared wilderness will find, over time, that the book has done something to their common life that it could not have done to any of them individually — that it has shaped the vocabulary they use to name their difficulty, the reference point they use to assess their obstacles, and the hope they carry forward into the thresholds that their shared journey will inevitably produce.

The specific formative power of the Kadesh Barnea account deserves additional emphasis for communities engaged in sustained reading. Unlike the complaint narratives, which press on the reader through accumulated recognition, the Kadesh Barnea account presses through a single concentrated moment of decision. Everything before it has been preparation. Everything after it is consequence. The twelve spies enter the land, spend forty days, return with evidence, and deliver their reports. The community responds. The sentence is pronounced. The entire arc of the second half of Numbers flows from the decision made at that specific moment by that specific community. The formative power of this for sustained reading is the power of the hinge — the recognition that there are moments in the life of every community when what appears to be an ordinary decision is actually the decision that determines the character of the next forty years. The community that has sat with the Kadesh Barnea account long enough to feel its weight will approach its own threshold moments differently — not necessarily with more courage than the ten spies, but with a clearer recognition of what kind of moment is actually occurring and what the specific stakes of the decision are. Numbers does not guarantee that communities will make better decisions at their thresholds because they have read it. It guarantees that communities who have read it will be less surprised by what the decision at the threshold actually costs.

Chapter 9

Reflection Questions

"The LORD is slow to anger, abounding in love and forgiving sin and rebellion. Yet he does not leave the guilty unpunished."
--- Numbers 14:18

Engaging Numbers

Numbers is not a book that can be read from a comfortable distance and received at its full weight. Its formation requires the willingness to bring one's own wilderness honestly to the text — to read the complaint narratives not as the failures of other people but as the mirror for one's own community's experience of what the long middle does to ordinary faith. The questions that follow are organized around the book's most pressing themes and are designed to generate that kind of honest engagement. They are not questions with comfortable answers. They are questions that grow more demanding the more honestly they are taken, and that yield more the more specifically they are applied to the actual conditions of the community or individual bringing them to the text.

These questions are designed to be returned to across different seasons of life and different stages of the wilderness journey. What they yield at the beginning of a long middle — when the wilderness is new and the faith is still relatively intact — will be different from what they yield in the middle of it, when the accumulated weight of ordinary days has begun to press on the community's capacity to believe. And what they yield on the other side of a wilderness, looking back at what it cost and what the

God who sustained the community through it proved to be capable of, will be different again. Numbers rewards repeated engagement across changing circumstances, and these questions are designed to facilitate that engagement.

On the Wilderness You Are In

Every serious community of faith is in some form of wilderness at any given moment — some version of the long middle between a genuine promise and its visible fulfillment, some stretch of ordinary days in which the destination is real but not yet arrived at and the question of whether to keep moving requires more faith than the current circumstances easily supply. Before engaging the specific questions Numbers generates, the foundational question must be asked honestly: where is your community's wilderness? Not in general — specifically. What is the specific thing that has been promised, genuinely believed, and not yet received? What is the specific form that the distance between promise and present reality takes in the actual texture of your community's daily life?

The wilderness that Numbers describes is not abstract. It is a specific terrain with specific hardships — water scarce at specific locations, food monotonous in a specific form, enemies real in specific territories, leadership challenged from specific directions. The honest engagement with the wilderness you are in requires the same specificity. Which dimension of your current circumstances is most pressing against your capacity to trust the God who called you to the journey you are on? Is it the duration — the sense that the wilderness has gone on longer than you expected and that the distance between your current position and the promised destination is not decreasing at the rate you anticipated? Is it the monotony — the sense that the provision, however real, has become so routine that it no longer functions as evidence of divine faithfulness? Is it the communal dimension —

the sense that the people around you are losing their ability to believe, and that their loss is beginning to press on your own?

Naming these dimensions of your specific wilderness with the specificity that Numbers itself models is not an exercise in complaint. It is the precondition for receiving what Numbers has to say about the territory you are actually in. The book cannot speak to a generalized spiritual difficulty. It speaks to specific wilderness conditions named honestly, and the reader who brings their specific conditions to it will find it addressing those conditions with a precision that vague spiritual encouragement cannot replicate.

On the Complaint You Are Carrying

Numbers gives the community's complaints more space than almost any other biblical book, and the space they are given is formative in its own right. The complaints are recorded with enough specificity that the reader who is carrying their own version of the same complaint will recognize it — the frustration with provision that feels inadequate to what was promised, the exhaustion with a journey that has gone on longer than expected, the anger at leadership that seems unable to move the community toward the destination it claims to be heading for. These are not the complaints of uniquely faithless people. They are the complaints of ordinary people in genuinely difficult circumstances, and Numbers invites the reader to own their version of them rather than project them onto the Israelites as evidence of a failure one's own community would not reproduce.

What is the specific complaint you are carrying about your current wilderness? Not the complaint you think you should be carrying, or the complaint that would be most spiritually presentable if you had to name it aloud — the actual complaint, the one that surfaces in the unguarded moments, the one that you have been managing rather than bringing honestly to the God you are supposed to be trusting. The Israelites' complaints in Numbers are memorable for their specificity: they named the fish and the leeks and the cucumbers they were missing. The specificity was not irrelevant to the complaint's significance. It was the evidence that the complaint was genuine rather than rhetorical, rooted in actual longing rather than performed dissatisfaction.

Numbers does not resolve the complaints by showing that the Israelites were wrong about the difficulty of the wilderness. The wilderness was genuinely hard. It resolves them — or rather, it shows what resolution requires — by demonstrating that the interpretation of the difficulty as divine abandonment was wrong. The God who was being doubted was the God who was providing the manna every morning and moving in the cloud every day. What would it mean to bring your specific complaint honestly — not the managed version, the actual version — and receive in response not the assurance that the difficulty is not real but the evidence that the God who has brought you this far is capable of bringing you the rest of the way?

On Your Own Kadesh Barnea

The Kadesh Barnea account is the most self-implicating passage in Numbers, and engaging it honestly requires the willingness to ask whether you have had your own version of it — your own moment when the promised destination was within reach, the obstacles were real and visible, and you chose the wilderness over the threshold because the obstacles looked larger than the God who had promised to help you cross them. This is not a question about exceptional spiritual failure. The ten spies were not exceptional failures. They were ordinary people making an ordinary human assessment of an extraordinary situation, and the assessment was not unreasonable given the available evidence. The cities were large. The inhabitants were powerful. The

Israelites, by their own assessment, looked like grasshoppers by comparison.

The question is not whether the obstacles at your threshold were real — they were — but whether the God who has brought you to that threshold has been factored into your assessment of your capacity to cross it. The Kadesh Barnea failure was not a failure of information. The Israelites knew about God's track record. They had experienced the plagues and the sea crossing and the Sinai theophany and the manna and the water from the rock. The failure was a failure of weighting — a decision, made at the most critical moment, to weight the evidence of the obstacles more heavily than the evidence of the God who had already overcome every previous obstacle. What threshold have you refused to cross, or are you currently refusing to cross, because the obstacles look larger than the God who is standing behind the promise that led you there?

The consequence of the Kadesh Barnea failure was forty years. Not as arbitrary punishment but as the working out of what the community's choice actually entailed — if you don't believe you can enter the land, you will not enter the land, and the journey will continue until the generation that couldn't believe has been replaced by the generation that can. What is your community currently wandering in that it could have entered if it had been willing to trust the God who brought it to the threshold? And what would it take to trust that God now — not to pretend the obstacles are smaller than they are, but to weight the evidence of who God has been more heavily than the evidence of what remains between the current position and the promised destination?

On Communal Doubt and the Caleb Question

Numbers presents the dynamics of communal doubt with unusual specificity, and the specificity has direct implications for how communities navigate the collective erosion of faith that extended wilderness periods consistently produce. The ten spies did not doubt in isolation. They expressed their doubt in a report delivered to the whole community, and the report did the work that doubt does when it is expressed collectively and authoritatively: it created in those who heard it the same fear it expressed, until what had been the perspective of ten became the mood of the entire community. The two who held a different view were not able to counter the weight of the ten, not because they were less persuasive but because the community's collective anxiety had already reached the point where it was more receptive to confirmation of its fears than to challenge of them.

The Caleb question for your community is the question about what role you are playing in the collective formation of its faith. Are you functioning as one of the ten — expressing your doubts about the promised destination in ways that contribute to the community's collective difficulty in believing — or as one of the two, offering the historically grounded, God-focused assessment that counters the weight of the collective fear with specific evidence of what the God who brought the community to this point has already demonstrated himself capable of? This is not a call to dishonest optimism. Caleb and Joshua did not deny that the land was inhabited by powerful people. They assessed those people from the reference point of the God who had already overcome more formidable obstacles than a fortified city. What would it mean to offer your community that kind of assessment from that kind of reference point, specifically and consistently, in the conversations that are currently shaping the collective mood?

On Leadership and the Distribution of Burden

Moses's prayer in chapter eleven — the moment when he tells God that the burden is too heavy and he cannot carry it alone — is one of the most honest leadership prayers in the entire Bible, and the question it generates for anyone in a leadership position is simple and searching: have you said this prayer? Not the managed version — the version that acknowledges that leadership is challenging while maintaining the presentation of adequate capacity — but the actual version, the version that Moses prayed, in which the honesty about the impossibility of the current situation was complete enough to include the request for release from it.

The divine response to Moses's prayer was not rebuke but provision: seventy elders to share the burden, the spirit of Moses distributed among them so that the weight being carried by one person could be distributed across many. The response models what genuine leadership support looks like from the divine side and asks what it looks like from the human side. What burden are you currently carrying in your leadership role that you were not designed to carry alone? What would it mean to name that burden with the specificity and the honesty that Moses named it — not as a confession of inadequacy but as the honest acknowledgment of a design feature that the current arrangement of your leadership responsibility is violating? And what would it take to allow the burden to be distributed in the way that Moses's burden was distributed — not abandoned, but shared across a broader base of genuine co-leadership?

On the Promise That Has Not Yet Arrived

The second generation of Numbers stands on the plains of Moab at the end of the book, holding the promise that their parents refused and preparing to receive what the previous generation could not believe was available to them. They are the image of every community that has inherited a genuine promise that has not yet been received in the form or on the timeline that was expected — that has been told what God intends and has been kept waiting by circumstances they did not create and consequences they did not earn. Before engaging the specific question this raises, the foundational question must be asked: what is the promise you are holding that has not yet arrived? Not in abstract — specifically. What did you believe God said about your future, your community's future, your vocation, your family? And how long have you been holding it, and in what form is it still present — as active expectation, as fading hope, or as the ember of something you once believed that you have been protecting against the wind of circumstances that has been threatening to extinguish it for longer than you expected?

The second generation did not receive the promise by recovering the faith of the first generation. They received it by being a different generation — formed in the wilderness by conditions that were not of their choosing, shaped by the provision of a God they had never experienced in any other form, carrying a promise they had inherited from parents who had refused it. Their readiness to receive was not heroic. It was the readiness of people who had never known anything other than the wilderness and who trusted the God of the wilderness because the God of the wilderness was the only God they had. What would it mean to receive the promise you are holding with that kind of straightforward, wilderness-formed trust — not the trust that has survived dramatic crisis, but the trust that has simply never stopped depending on the God who has been providing the manna every morning?

Questions for Continued Engagement

These questions are a beginning rather than a completion. Numbers is designed to generate more searching engagement the more honestly it is read — not because it is obscure but because the wilderness it describes is deep, and depth yields more to each return than any single engagement can draw out. The reader who returns to Numbers in six months, from a different position in their own wilderness, will find that the questions have not been answered and set aside but have deepened and become more specific, because the wilderness being brought to them has changed and because different episodes in the narrative have become newly urgent in the new circumstances.

The most important thing about these questions is not that they be answered definitively but that they be taken seriously with the honesty that Numbers itself models. Numbers does not flatter its readers. It presents the failure of the wilderness generation with enough specificity and enough accuracy that the reader who engages it honestly will recognize their own community's version of the same failure rather than congratulating themselves on their superiority to those who failed. The formation that this honest recognition produces — the realistic, resilient, wilderness-tested faith that knows what the long middle costs and what the God who sustains the community through it is capable of — is what Numbers has always been designed to produce in those willing to bring their actual wilderness to it rather than the acceptable version.

A final suggestion for continued engagement: read Numbers alongside whatever other account of extended difficulty and divine faithfulness the community is living through or has recently lived through. The wilderness narrative of Numbers is most powerful when it is brought into direct conversation with specific contemporary experience — not as a proof text for the conclusion that God is faithful, but as the extended, specific, honest account of what divine faithfulness looks like from inside conditions that do not feel like faithfulness, set alongside the extended, specific, honest account of what the contemporary community's wilderness has felt like from inside. The conversation between these two accounts — the ancient one and the contemporary one — is where the deepest formation happens. Not in the application of the ancient account's conclusions to the contemporary situation, but in the honest recognition that the conditions are not as different as they initially appear, and that the God who was faithful in the ancient wilderness is the same God who is present in the contemporary one. This is what it means to read Numbers as the living word it was always designed to be.

Chapter 10

Five Lessons

"Do not be afraid of the people of the land, because we will devour them. Their protection is gone, but the LORD is with us."
--- Numbers 14:9

Five Lessons from Numbers

Numbers has been forming communities of faith across three thousand years because the territory it describes is territory that every generation of the covenant community inhabits in some form. The wilderness between promise and fulfillment does not belong only to the ancient Israelites. It is the common experience of every community that has received a genuine calling, set out toward a genuine destination, and discovered that the journey is harder, longer, and more demanding than the initial calling suggested. The book that records the most sustained failure in Israel's history is also the book that most honestly addresses the conditions that every subsequent generation of that history has navigated, and the lessons it presses on those who engage it seriously do not diminish with the passage of time.

The five lessons that follow are not a summary of Numbers's content. They are a distillation of the most persistent and most demanding things the book asks of those who receive it — the things that remain pressing after all the historical context has been provided, all the structural features have been explained, and all the specific episodes have been examined in their original setting. They are the lessons that remain when the reader has finished understanding Numbers and is left with the question it has been building toward from its first census to its final encampment on the plains of Moab: will you trust the God who has brought you this far to bring you the rest of the way?

Lesson One: The Wilderness Is Not the Enemy

The first and most counterintuitive lesson of Numbers is the one that the wilderness-as-formation theme presses most directly: the wilderness is not primarily an obstacle to be escaped or a punishment to be endured. It is the space in which the community is being formed for what it has been promised. The generation that died in the wilderness died there because they refused to trust the God who was trying to lead them through it to their destination. The generation that grew up in the wilderness entered the promised land as a more coherently organized, more legally sophisticated, more covenantally formed community than the generation that had left Egypt. The wilderness years were not wasted years. They were formation years, and the formation they produced was the formation the community needed in order to receive what had been promised.

This first lesson is among the most practically significant contributions Numbers makes to communities navigating extended difficulty, and it is the one that is most consistently missed by communities that treat their wilderness as a problem to be solved rather than a context to be inhabited faithfully. The community that is organized primarily around escaping the wilderness — that measures its spiritual health by how quickly it can move from the difficulty of the present to the comfort of the arrival it is expecting — will find the wilderness more disorienting than the community that understands the wilderness as the place where the God who has called it to its destination is also forming it for the reception of that destination.

Receiving this lesson practically means developing the capacity to ask the formation question in the middle of the wilderness rather than only in retrospect: what is being produced here that could not be produced anywhere else? What is being revealed about the community's actual commitments, its actual capacity, its actual relationship to the God it claims to follow, that the comfortable circumstances it left would never have surfaced? What is being stripped away that needed to be stripped — the dependencies on conditions rather than on God, the confidence in its own resources rather than in the one who called it, the attachment to a way of life that the calling required leaving behind? The wilderness is not comfortable. But Numbers insists that it is purposeful, and that the purpose is not punishment but preparation.

The practical test of whether a community has received this first lesson is visible in how it talks about its own wilderness. The community that describes its difficult season primarily in terms of loss — what it no longer has, what it is no longer able to do, what has been taken from it — has not yet received the formation dimension of the wilderness. The community that can name, alongside the genuine losses, the specific things being produced and revealed and stripped away that the previous season could not have produced — that community has begun to inhabit the wilderness on the terms that Numbers commends.

Lesson Two: Divine Faithfulness Outlasts Human Failure

The second lesson of Numbers is the one its overall narrative arc demonstrates most conclusively: the faithfulness of God outlasts the failure of the community he has called. The wilderness generation failed comprehensively and consistently across forty years of documented complaint, rebellion, and refusal. And the God they were failing was the God who kept sending the manna every morning, kept moving in the cloud every day, kept preserving the community through the consequences of its own choices, and ultimately kept the promise to Abraham by bringing the next generation to the threshold that the previous one had refused. The faithfulness was not conditional on the faithfulness of those it was directed toward. It was grounded in the character of the one who committed to it, and that character did not change with the community's performance.

The practical implication of this second lesson is simultaneously the most comforting and the most destabilizing claim Numbers makes. Comforting, because it means that the accumulated failures of a community — the seasons of complaint and unbelief, the Kadesh Barnea moments when the threshold was refused, the Baal Peor episodes when the community embraced what it had been called away from — are not the final word about a community whose God has committed himself to keeping a promise that did not depend on the community's merit in the first place. The promise was made to Abraham before any of his descendants had demonstrated the capacity to receive it, and it has been kept across millennia of the kind of performance the wilderness generation delivered.

Destabilizing, because it means that the community cannot use the certainty of divine faithfulness as a reason to treat its own faithfulness casually. The wilderness generation discovered that divine faithfulness includes the faithfulness to work out the consequences of communal failure — that the God who does not abandon the community also does not pretend the community's choices have no consequences. The manna arrived every morning and the sentence of forty years was fully served. Both are expressions of the same divine faithfulness, and communities that receive the comforting dimension without the destabilizing one have not received the second lesson at the depth at which Numbers presses it.

The second lesson also has a specific implication for how communities understand the relationship between their own faithfulness and the faithfulness of the God they are serving. Communities that are primarily motivated by the desire to secure divine favor through demonstrated faithfulness have organized their spiritual life around an incentive structure that Numbers systematically dismantles. The community that is faithful because it believes that faithfulness produces favorable outcomes will find its faithfulness tested most severely precisely in the seasons when the outcomes do not arrive as expected. The community that is faithful because it has received the second lesson of Numbers — that the God it is serving has already demonstrated, across forty years of wilderness, that his commitment to the community does not depend on the community's performance — will find a more durable motivation for faithfulness than outcome management can provide.

Lesson Three: Complaints Diagnose the Heart

The third lesson of Numbers is the one the complaint narratives press most directly: the specific content of a community's complaints reveals the specific location of its trust failures. The Israelites' complaints in Numbers are not random expressions of general dissatisfaction. They are diagnostic — they reveal, with considerable precision, where the community's trust in the God who brought it out of Egypt was organized around outcomes rather than around the character of the one who called it. The complaint about food revealed that their trust in divine provision extended only as far as the quality of the provision met their remembered standard. The complaint about leadership revealed that their trust in divinely appointed authority extended only as far as that authority was producing outcomes they preferred. The refusal at Kadesh Barnea revealed that their trust in divine power extended only as far as the obstacles between them and the promised destination were small enough not to require it.

The diagnostic function of complaints means that honest engagement with the community's actual complaints — not the managed versions, but the real ones — is one of the most useful instruments of self-examination available to communities of faith in the wilderness. The content of what a community complains about, taken seriously and examined honestly, will consistently reveal the specific points at which the community's trust in God is organized around conditions rather than around character — the points at which the community is trusting God to perform in a specific way rather than trusting the God who performs as he chooses because of who he is.

This third lesson is not a call to suppress complaints or to perform contentment that is not genuinely felt. Moses prayed his actual complaint in chapter eleven, and God responded with provision rather than rebuke. The lesson is rather that complaints, honestly brought and honestly examined, are data rather than simply expressions of distress — that the community willing to ask what its complaints reveal about the location of its trust failures will find them pointing toward the specific work that the wilderness years are designed to accomplish. The community that manages its complaints rather than examining them will find the wilderness longer and less productive than the community that brings them honestly and receives from them the diagnostic information they were designed to provide.

Lesson Four: The Mission Belongs to God, Not the Leader

The fourth lesson of Numbers is the one that Moses's disqualification at Meribah presses most directly: the mission is God's property, and no leader's indispensability to it is greater than the terms on which they were appointed to serve it. Moses led the community faithfully for decades, interceded for it repeatedly, bore the weight of its leadership at enormous personal cost, and was ultimately disqualified by a single moment of representative failure — speaking as though the water came from his own power rather than from the God he was supposed to be representing. The disqualification was not a proportional punishment for a minor offense. It was the consistent application of the principle that the closer one stands to the divine mission in a representative capacity, the more completely one's actions must correspond to the character of the one being represented.

The mission's independence from the leader is the most pastorally significant dimension of this fourth lesson. Moses does not enter the promised land. Joshua does. The mission continues, the promise is kept, and the land is entered — by someone else, on behalf of a community that Moses led to the threshold but did not cross. This is Numbers' most direct word to every leader who has poured themselves into a mission that they believe requires their specific continued leadership: the mission does not depend on you. It depends on the God who called you to it, and if your chapter in the mission ends before the mission is complete — by failure, by exhaustion, by the natural limits of a human life span, or by the kind of disqualification that Meribah represents — the mission continues under the leadership of the next person God appoints.

The commissioning of Joshua in Numbers twenty-seven is the practical enactment of this fourth lesson, and it is worth sitting with for longer than most leadership accounts allow. Moses does not negotiate his disqualification. He does not campaign for reconsideration. He asks God to appoint a successor so that the community will not be like sheep without a shepherd, lays hands on Joshua publicly, and transfers to him the authority the mission requires. The gesture is both the acknowledgment of personal failure and the prioritization of the mission over the leader's attachment to it. The capacity to do this — to invest the next generation of leadership with the authority the mission needs rather than hoarding that authority to the end — is the leadership wisdom that Numbers commends through Moses's example and that is as rare and as necessary in contemporary leadership as it was in the wilderness.

Lesson Five: The Second Chance Is Real

The fifth and most hopeful lesson of Numbers is the one that the second census and the second generation embody most completely: the God of the wilderness gives second chances. Not as the softening of consequences that have not yet been fully experienced, but as the renewed possibility that exists on the other side of consequences that have been fully and honestly worked through. The first generation's consequences were real. The forty years were served. The generation died, one by one, across four decades of wilderness wandering, until the last of them had gone and a new generation stood in their place. And on the other side of all of that, the promise was still standing — as fresh and as specific and as available as it had been when the first generation refused it at Kadesh Barnea.

The second chance in Numbers is not a reset that erases the history of the failure that made it necessary. The second generation knew what their parents had done and what it had cost. The forty years of their childhood were the direct consequence of a failure they did not personally commit. They had grown up in the wilderness because the generation before them had preferred it to the threshold. And yet they stood at the threshold themselves — not with the innocence of those who have never failed, but with the readiness of those who have lived inside the consequences of failure long enough to know exactly what the refusal to trust costs, and who are therefore positioned to choose differently at their own threshold than their parents chose at theirs.

This is the most practically sustaining word that Numbers speaks to communities carrying the weight of their own accumulated failures. The promise did not expire when the first generation refused it. It waited. The God who made it kept it present, kept it specific, kept it available, across forty years of the first generation's dying and the second generation's growing up, until a community stood at the threshold that was capable of receiving what could not be received before. For communities that are currently living inside the consequences of past failures — navigating the long middle that their own Kadesh Barnea moments made necessary — Numbers offers the most honest and the most grounded hope available: the second chance is real, the promise is still standing, and the God who made it has demonstrated across the entire wilderness narrative that he is capable of bringing the community to its destination on the other side of any failure the community has managed to produce.

The community that takes Numbers seriously enough to let it press these five lessons into the specific texture of its actual wilderness will find that the book's formation is not something that can be acquired in a single reading or even a single season of engagement. It accumulates. The reader who returns to the first lesson — the wilderness is not the enemy — after a year of navigating a difficult institutional season will find it saying something they could not have received at the beginning of the season, because the season has given them the specific experience that the lesson requires to land at its full weight. The reader who returns to the fifth lesson — the second chance is real — after living through the consequences of a significant failure will find it saying something that no amount of pre-failure theological knowledge could have prepared them to receive. This is the character of the formation that the five lessons of Numbers produce: not the mastery of content that can be applied at will to any situation, but the deepening of understanding that only the wilderness produces in those willing to stay in it long enough to discover that the God who called them there is still present, still providing, still faithful, and still committed to bringing them to the destination the promise named. The manna arrives in the morning. The cloud moves in the day. The promise stands at every threshold. These are the five lessons of Numbers distilled to their simplest and their most enduring form.

What Numbers Has Given to the World

The influence of Numbers on the history of communities of faith is both more extensive and more indirect than the influence of the books that flank it in the Torah. It has given the tradition its most sustained and most honest portrait of communal failure in the wilderness, and that portrait has functioned as the primary biblical resource for every subsequent generation navigating its own version of the long middle. Paul reaches for it when writing to the Corinthians about the dangers of spiritual complacency. The author of Hebrews reaches for it when warning about the hardening of the heart that sustained unbelief produces. Every tradition of desert spirituality — from the desert fathers and mothers of the third and fourth centuries to the contemplative traditions that developed from their witness — has drawn on the wilderness narrative of Numbers as the primary map for understanding what the encounter with God in conditions of deprivation produces and why it produces it.

The Balaam oracles have given the tradition some of its most important messianic poetry — the star out of Jacob and the scepter rising from Israel that the Magi of the Matthew nativity narrative are understood to be following across centuries of interpretive connection. The daughters of Zelophehad episode has given every tradition of legal development within religious communities a model for how law develops in response to specific cases that expose the limits of existing provisions. The Korah rebellion has given every tradition of religious authority a mirror for examining the difference between legitimate challenge and the use of true theological claims to override specific divine appointments. Numbers is not the most read book in the Torah. But its contributions to the tradition that has read it across three thousand years are woven through that tradition in ways that would leave it significantly impoverished if removed.

The Enduring Questions

The questions that Numbers raises cannot be finally answered by any community in any era, and they will therefore continue to press themselves on every community that takes the book seriously. They are questions about the interpretation of difficulty — whether the wilderness conditions of the present are being read as divine abandonment or as divine testing, and what the difference between those two interpretations produces in the community's capacity to keep moving toward its destination. They are questions about the management of communal doubt — whether the community is being shaped primarily by the voices that confirm its fears or by the voices that assess its situation from the reference point of what God has already demonstrated himself capable of. They are questions about leadership — whether those who bear the responsibility for moving the community forward are doing so in a way that represents the God who called them or in a way that represents their own investment in the outcomes they are working toward.

These questions are currently being asked with unusual urgency in the contemporary world, because the communities of faith that are navigating the most extended wildernesses of institutional decline, cultural skepticism, and the accumulated consequences of past failures are precisely the communities that most need what Numbers has always offered: the honest account of what the wilderness does to ordinary communities, the equally honest account of what the God who is in the wilderness with those communities does with their failures, and the sustaining assurance that the promise has not expired and the second chance is real.

The Permanent Invitation

The invitation that Numbers extends across its thirty-six chapters is the invitation that the second census embodies and the plains-of-Moab encampment enacts: come and stand at the threshold, and trust the God who has brought you here to bring you the rest of the way. It is the invitation that the first generation received and refused, that the second generation received and accepted, and that every subsequent generation has received in the form appropriate to its own circumstances and its own threshold.

Numbers was not written for communities that have their wilderness behind them and their promised destination already received. It was written for communities in motion — imperfectly, fitfully, complaint-punctuated, leadership-challenged, collectively-doubting motion toward a destination that the God who promised it has committed himself to delivering. The manna is real. The cloud is moving. The promise is standing. And the God who has been faithful across every wilderness his people have ever navigated is the God who stands at the threshold of the next one, asking the question that Numbers has always been asking: will you trust me to bring you in?

The community that has received Numbers honestly — that has sat with its complaint narratives long enough to recognize its own complaints in them, that has asked the Kadesh Barnea question honestly enough to admit the uncertainty of its answer, that has received the second census as the testimony it is to a God whose promise outlasts the generation that refused it — is the community best positioned to answer that question with something other than the response the first generation gave. Not because it has achieved a level of faith that places it beyond the wilderness generation's failure, but because it knows what the wilderness costs and what the God who walks through it is capable of. The manna will be adequate. The cloud will continue moving. The promise will be kept. This is what forty years in the wilderness established beyond reasonable doubt, and what every subsequent generation of the community that inherited the account has had the opportunity to discover for itself. Numbers keeps this testimony alive across the millennia because the wilderness it describes is the wilderness that never entirely ends, and the God it describes is the God who never entirely leaves.

What Numbers ultimately asks of the reader is not theological sophistication or historical knowledge or the specific skills of biblical interpretation, though all of these help. What it asks is the same thing it asked of the wilderness generation and the same thing it asked of the second generation standing on the plains of Moab: the willingness to bring the actual wilderness — the real conditions, the genuine complaints, the honest assessment of the obstacles at the threshold — and to receive from the God who is present in it the specific provision that the specific conditions require. The manna was not the provision the community wanted. It was the provision the community needed to survive the journey. The cloud was not moving in the direction the community preferred. It was moving in the direction that the promise required. The forty years were not the timeline the community had planned for. They were the timeline that the community's own failure at Kadesh Barnea made necessary, and the God who organized that timeline was the same God who was moving through it with the community every day of its duration. This is the testimony that Numbers preserves and that every generation that inherits it has the opportunity to prove for itself: that the God of the wilderness is adequate to the wilderness, that the manna arrives in the morning, and that the cloud moves toward the destination even when the community would prefer to stay where it is. Come and see.

Closing Reflection

*"The LORD bless you and keep you; the LORD make his face
shine on you and be gracious to you; the LORD turn his face
toward you and give you peace."*
--- Numbers 6:24-26

Numbers has endured because the wilderness it describes has not
gone away. Every generation of the covenant community has
inhabited some version of the long middle this book maps — the
stretch of ordinary days between the genuine promise and its
visible fulfillment, in which the question of whether to keep
moving toward the destination presses itself on the community in
the specific forms that the community's specific circumstances
generate. The specific hardships change. The manna arrives in
different forms. The cloud moves in directions that the
community does not always find intuitive. The Kadesh Barnea
moments come at different thresholds and look different in
different eras. But the underlying territory — the long middle, the
sustained test of whether the God who has brought the
community this far can be trusted to bring it the rest of the way
— is the same territory that the wilderness generation navigated
and failed in, and that every subsequent generation has navigated
in its own form.

What gives Numbers its lasting power is not the drama of its
most spectacular episodes, though the fire that devoured Nadab
and Abihu and the earth that swallowed Korah and the bronze
serpent lifted up in the wilderness are among the most vivid
images in the Torah. It is the sustained, unflinching honesty with
which the book inhabits the space between the spectacular
moments — the forty years of ordinary wilderness days in which
the manna arrived and the community complained and the cloud

moved and the journey continued and the promise remained standing despite everything the community did to test its durability. The wilderness is long. The manna is real. The complaints are understandable. The faithfulness is unbroken. Numbers holds all four of these truths simultaneously and refuses to allow any one of them to crowd out the others, and the result is the most honest portrait of covenant life in the long middle that the biblical canon contains.

One of the most characteristic features of Numbers, observed across the entire history of its reception, is its resistance to being received as a comfortable book. Every generation that has approached it hoping to find encouragement without self-implication has found the wilderness generation staring back at them with uncomfortable familiarity — their complaints recognizable, their fears understandable, their failure at Kadesh Barnea not the exceptional wickedness of uniquely faithless people but the ordinary failure of ordinary people who could not quite bring themselves to trust the God who had already done everything he had promised to do up to that point. The book does not allow the reader to observe the Israelites' failure from a safe distance. It presses the Kadesh Barnea question on every reader: at your own threshold, with your own obstacles, with your own evidence of what God has already done — would you have done differently? Most honest readers find that the answer is less certain than they would prefer.

Numbers was written for a community that needed to understand its own history honestly before it could move forward faithfully. The wilderness generation's failure was not something the subsequent tradition was inclined to suppress or sentimentalize. It was preserved in detail, with the specificity of actual complaint and actual rebellion and actual consequence, because the community that inherited the account needed to know what the wilderness does to ordinary faith and what the God who walks through the wilderness with his people is capable of doing with their failure. The second generation that stood on the plains of Moab at the end of the book was the generation that had grown up inside those consequences — that had inherited the account of the first generation's failure not as a remote historical record but as the explanation of their own childhood, the reason for the wilderness years that were the only life they had known. They moved toward the threshold with the knowledge of what refusal cost, and that knowledge was part of what prepared them to trust the God they were crossing into the land under.

Reading Numbers well across a lifetime — returning to the complaint narratives in different wilderness seasons, to the Kadesh Barnea account at different thresholds, to the Balaam oracles when the community needs to hear itself described from outside, to the second census when hope has been beaten down long enough that the prospect of a fresh beginning is the most sustaining word available — produces a specific and irreplaceable formation. Not the heroic faith that has never doubted and never complained, but the realistic, durable, wilderness-tested faith that has looked at forty years of documented failure in the most comprehensive wilderness narrative in the Torah and found in them not the absence of divine faithfulness but its most sustained and most searching demonstration. The manna arrived every morning for forty years. The cloud moved every day for forty years. The promise was kept across every failure the community managed to produce. This is the knowledge that sustained engagement with Numbers builds into the community that returns to it honestly and repeatedly, and it is the knowledge that the wilderness most requires.

The invitation Numbers extends is the same invitation it has always extended, from the organized expectation of the Sinai departure to the renewed readiness of the plains-of-Moab encampment. Come and inhabit the wilderness honestly. Bring the actual complaint, not the managed version. Face the Kadesh Barnea question at your own threshold with the specific evidence of what God has already done as your primary reference point rather than the specific evidence of the obstacles that remain. Receive the formation that the long middle produces as purposeful rather than merely punishing. Trust the God of the second census, who turns to the next generation after the consequences of the first generation's failure have been fully worked out and prepares them to receive what their parents refused. The wilderness is long. The promise is real. And the God who has been with the community through every day of the journey it has traveled so far is the God who was with the wilderness generation for forty years in the desert and who stands now at every threshold his people have reached, asking the question that Numbers has always been asking: will you trust me to bring you in?

The reader who closes Numbers and sets it aside has not yet finished with it. Numbers is a book that follows the reader into the circumstances that follow the reading — into the specific wilderness that the reading has clarified, into the specific threshold that the reading has named, into the specific conversations with the Caleb and ten-spies voices in the community that the reading has made newly urgent. The formation it produces is not complete at the last page. It is the formation of a community in motion, and the motion continues after the reading ends. The wilderness generation's story is finished, their sentence served, their place taken by a generation that could receive what they refused. The reader's story is not finished. The reader's wilderness continues. The reader's threshold is still ahead. And the God who kept the promise for the second generation, after everything the first generation did to test whether the promise was keepable, is the God who will keep it for the reader — through the length of the wilderness still to be traveled, through the obstacles still standing between the current position and the destination, through whatever the reader's own version of Kadesh Barnea turns out to require. The manna will be there in the morning. The cloud will be moving. Come and see.

The Bible for Modern Life Series

This book is part of **The Bible for Modern Life** series—an ongoing collection that explores the meaning, historical setting, and message of individual books of Scripture.

Each volume looks closely at the biblical text to help readers understand what it meant in its original context and how its truths still apply to life today.

The goal is simple: to help modern readers engage more deeply with the Bible—one book at a time.

— Samuel Whitaker